THE ORAL COMMUNICATOR
HIS ROLE AND FUNCTION

by

ALBERT TEPPER
PAUL A. ROMAN

Department of Speech
San Diego City College
San Diego, California

Illustrated by

DANIEL D. LEAVITT

Burgess Publishing Company
426 South Sixth Street • Minneapolis, Minn. 55415

PN4121
T42

DEDICATION

As an expression of appreciation for the patience and encouragement of our wives during the preparation of this project, this book is affectionately dedicated to MARIAN and MARJORIE.

PREFACE

A primary goal of *The Oral Communicator: His Role and Function* shall be to present fundamental principles and theories which apply to speaking occasions from limited audience techniques to mass communication skills. Adult experiences and opportunities for increased efficiency in these experiences will be emphasized. The language will strive to be non-technical yet comprehensive and intelligible to the total range of abilities present in an average community college classroom.

Having a combined total of over twenty-five years teaching experience in adult and junior college education, as well as many years of practical experience in the field of public address and oral communications, we feel especially well qualified in addressing ourselves to this project. The authors are currently on the staff of the San Diego City College. Mr. Tepper is the chairman of the Speech Department and director of the Forensics program. Mr. Roman has served as the chairman of the Radio-Television Department and acting Dean of the Arts and Sciences Division.

ACKNOWLEDGEMENTS

Any social being is the net result of his reactions to his perceptions and experiences. An author, as any communicator, is influenced by many subtle forces. It is, therefore, often impossible to identify the precise influences which have contributed to the composite whole. The exact source for most of the ideas in this text book is lost in the maze of many years of exposure to teachers, students, and text books.

In particular, the authors feel a sense of indebtedness to Alan H. Monroe[1], whose texts on public address have influenced generations of students and instructors. More recently the works of Charles T. Brown and Charles Van Riper[2] in the field of semantics, and Carl H. Weaver and Warren L. Strausbaugh[3] in the area of Oral Communications theory have had a significant influence on the author's current thought.

We would further like to express our appreciation to the hundreds of students who have passed through our classes and have contributed so much to *our* education in the field of oral communications over the years.

1. Monroe, Alan H., *Monroe's Principles of Speech,* Chicago, Scott, Foresman and Company, 1945.
2. Brown, Charles T. and Charles Van Riper, *Speech and Man,* New Jersey, Prentice Hall Inc., 1966.
3. Weaver, Carl H. and Warren L. Strausbaugh, *Fundamentals of Speech Communications,* New York, American Book Co., 1964.

TABLE OF CONTENTS

Page

INTRODUCTION

The community junior college or two-year college as an institution has within the past decade taken on increased importance within the realm of higher education in the United States. Not only has the enrollment annually set new records, but the number of schools being constructed to house that enrollment is growing monthly. California, New York, Florida, Arizona, and Illinois are only five of the states that are leading the nation in providing education beyond the high school for ALL students who can profit from instruction.

A portion of the growth in enrollment in junior colleges is due to the increased enrollment pattern in the four-year institutions and the shift in emphasis to research and graduate studies in advanced education. The junior college has taken upon itself the responsibility for meeting the needs of the entire community by educating students in vocational and technical subjects as well as academic transfer areas. No longer does college mean simply academic studies as it has in the past.

With this continued emphasis being universally placed upon education beyond high school, the community junior college has expanded its offerings to include a continuum of courses from basic skill courses in vocational areas to activities and classes for the leisure time of the retired citizen and, finally, to the transfer classes for the most able students. In a true sense, the comprehensive community college has become all things to all people.

The heterogeneous nature of the junior college student body is a distinct advantage to the oral communications classes. In few other disciplines can the slow student acquire or profit so much from association with and observance of the better student as in the area of communication.

The majority of college texts prepared in the area of public address or oral communications have in the past been prepared for the specialized training of a small percentage of the college population. Texts are written for persons anticipating their role as a public speaker: lawyers, politicians, educators, clergymen, or other professional persons. Still other texts are written as academic exercises by college professors seeking to extend the knowledge of public address and rhetoric through historical or traditional studies. The vast majority of these texts disregard the student who simply wishes to *learn how to communicate* with individuals or groups in real life situations, such as P.T.A. functions, union meetings, or social gatherings.

An oral communication text for the community college student should provide the slow student with guidelines for developing and communicating his thoughts and ideas effectively, as well as providing the academically oriented student with the background necessary for advanced work in public address or rhetoric. It is the intent of THE ORAL COMMUNICATOR: HIS ROLE AND FUNC-TION to provide for these extremes while achieving the goal of more effective communication for all.

CHAPTER ONE
THE ORAL COMMUNICATOR

The next time you find yourself in a crowd, look around. You'll be amazed to discover how many different kinds of people you can see: some are fat, others thin; there are those with long hair, others with short hair or none at all; you'll see blondes (real or otherwise), brunettes, and redheads; some people have fair skins, others are dark; there are long, short, or remade noses; blue, green, or snapping black eyes . . . in short, people in most physical aspects are not alike. In other respects, however, people are very much alike. We share similar goals and have common desires. Most of us are interested in raising our families, earning a good living, working at a job we enjoy, meeting new people and making friends. We also share in common the need to achieve some form of success in life. Each of us has his own idea of success and the form it will take . . . it may take the form of service to society, achieving a particular economic level, or possibly your idea of success may be in discovering the cure for the common cold. Regardless of the form, success is a necessary part of a full and happy life. In most cases, special equipment is necessary for success in reaching a desired goal; the gold miner needs his shaker for panning gold, the musician needs his instrument to perform, the football player needs padding and equipment to succeed. We need the right tools for everything that we attempt if we are to be successful.

If you were offered a tool which could help you to make *your idea* of success possible, would you be interested? It is the purpose of this book and the course in which you are now enrolled to provide you with such a tool. A tool, however, is no better than the person using it; practice not only improves the skill of the user, but the product becomes far more valuable.

We live today in a world which, to a large extent, is controlled and directed by *words*: radio, television and the movies influence our attitudes; books, newspapers, and magazines guide our thinking; teachers, ministers, and parents seek to guide and direct us; and all of these use words to accomplish their aims. From the time you wake in the morning until you go to bed at night, and from the moment you are born until the time you die, you are constantly bombarded with and influenced by words; words written and read, spoken and listened to.

If you stopped to think of the millions of words you are exposed to in the course of your lifetime it would stagger your imagination. The sad fact is, that in spite of the number of words in our lives, most of us do not use even a portion of these easily, effectively, or properly. This book proposes to provide you with the tool of effective oral communication . . . the tool of using words.

Most of us have had few, if any, experiences in our lives when we have felt the need or have been called upon to speak before large audiences, but ALL of us are involved in speaking situations before small groups, on the job, in the classrooms, at church gatherings, at social situations, only to name a few. On many such occasions we are called upon to communicate our ideas or to support others in their ideas.

Mark Twain once noted that most young men at age seventeen are quick to admit that their parents are not very bright , . . but by the time they reach the age of twenty-one they are amazed to discover how much *their parents* have learned. This story shows one of the problems which people face in working and living together, the lack of communication. Teenagers can't talk with their parents and married couples often end up in divorce courts as a result of their lack of communication. Job difficulties often result from problems associated with lack of communication between employers and employees. Shocking headlines in our daily newspapers clearly demonstrate the results of poor communications between races, people, and nations.

We hear a lot about this word COMMUNICATION, but like many other words which we use, it is not generally understood. Before attempting to learn about effective communication, there should be some mutual agreement about its meaning.

WHAT IS COMMUNICATION

Communication can best be defined as a signaling and receiving of thoughts and ideas between two or more individuals. When you write a letter and receive no answer, you have not communicated since you have no way of knowing how your thoughts, ideas and opinions affected the person to whom you sent the letter. It becomes a communication only when you receive an answer. The same thing applies to oral communications. A parent who refuses to listen, a teacher who is unaware of his students' feelings, a marriage where ideas are not shared; all are examples of communication failure.

Effective communication is a means of sharing, relating and better understanding what we as individuals acquire in the way of information and knowledge of the world about us. Primitive people communicated by means of pictures; young lovers (and old lovers as well) communicate with a look or a glance. A parent can speak volumes to a naughty child with a frown or a shake of the head. But the method of communication which most of us use is a verbal expression of our thoughts, ideas, and feelings.

Learning to speak is not difficult. Learning to speak *well*, on the other hand, can be a trying experience. Most of us begin to develop the skills involved in speech as soon as we are born. An infant is learning to talk from the moment he utters his first loud cry announcing to the world that he has arrived. A child's grunts and gurgles, and his later babbling and vocal play all prepare him for future speech. As we grow and develop we discover that words can be used to manipulate parents and peers; words are a means of satisfying our needs and they allow us to express our feelings and emotions. When we think of speech we often think only of vocalizing sounds and words, but many other factors come into play when we think of communication. An important requirement of effective communication is that the person communicating should have beliefs, convictions, and opinions worthy of sharing with others. You must choose your words carefully as you attempt to stimulate another person to think and feel as you do. *Your success as a communicator is measured by the amount of success which you have in using words to shape ideas which will cause your listener to create similar or like thoughts in his mind.* Your co-communicators' preformed attitudes and opinions, his previous experiences, and his reaction to you as an individual all play a part in the communication act.

Communication is an interaction between people. Communication is and should be a two way street; there must be give and take, presentation and reception, sending and sensing. Your ability to sense and respond to the messages and signals of others serves to help you determine if, and to what degree, you have achieved effective communication.

WHY COMMUNICATE

Learning to mean what you say and to say what you mean is a very satisfying experience. By communicating effectively with other people you will be opening up new horizons. As a conscientious sender of ideas you will become more aware of your responsibility for having something of worth to say. As an effective receiver, you will be in a position to acquire new and interesting information and knowledge.

An old fable tells us that we were given two eyes and two ears but only one mouth because it was meant that we should listen and see twice as much as we spoke. This is good advice for beginning speakers. The more time we spend in listening to others and in seeing (observing carefully), the better qualified we become to communicate when it is our time to speak up. To be a full partner in the give-and-take process of communication you are going to be required to continually grow and develop as a thinking, well-informed person.

As a result of your interest in communication, you should discover and nurture a new interest in the world around you. The news of your community and the world, movies, plays, television, your reading, your hobbies, your social and special interests all will take on new meaning when you realize that these interests are a source of information and knowledge with which you meet your share of the responsibility for communication.

IT CAN HAPPEN TO YOU

There is no special magic involved in becoming a successful speaker. Learning to speak well is no harder than learning any other skill. If you want to learn to play a guitar, you must plan on long hours of practice. Bowlers learn to achieve high scores by bowling often, golfers achieve low scores through many hours spent on the practice tee and on the fairways, and speakers learn to speak well in much the same way . . . PRACTICE.

As in any skill development, just practicing is not enough; you must learn *what* to practice and *how* to practice so you are not just re-inforcing your existing bad habits.

There are a few simple rules which you should become aware of which will help you look, feel, and be more comfortable as you speak:

BE POISED   Your audience reacts to both what they see and what they hear. If you look confident and sure of yourself your audience will have more faith in what you say.

LOOK AT YOUR AUDIENCE   As you speak to people it is important that you look *at them* to determine the effect you are having *on them.* A common fault the beginning speaker has is avoiding his listeners' eyes by looking over their heads, at the floor, or past them.

Most of us are not too uncomfortable when speaking to one friendly person. When we are speaking to one person we can tell if they are listening to what we say and if they agree or disagree by watching the expression on his face. Look at individuals as you speak and think of them as friends. The speech then becomes a conversation with people and not a performance before an audience.

HAVE SOMETHING TO SAY   There are few experiences more agonizing than seeing an empty speaker attempt to pour himself out before a full house. To be an effective speaker you must have something worthwhile and interesting to say. Unless you have something significant to say and are interested in your subject, you can hardly expect your listeners to be interested.

BE INTERESTING   Your voice is the major indicator of your feelings and attitudes toward your topic. A vital, interested, sincere speaker must show his interest by having an interesting voice. Speak slowly and distinctly. Don't rush. Remember that the listener must have time to hear, digest, and react to your ideas.

SUMMARY

We have in this chapter talked very briefly about some of the steps which you as a speaker must take in becoming a more effective communicator, and the choice of the word "steps" has been intentional. Before an infant learns to take his first hesitant steps, he learns to crawl. He then progresses to the stage of being helped and guided in the mastery of moving about in an upright position. Finally comes that proud day when the infant is able to take the first faltering steps on his own. In the process there are always setbacks and sitbacks as well. The same can be expected in developing skill in effective communication. When you are just beginning to acquire your skill in speaking you must expect to make mistakes. As with the infant learning to walk, there will be times when you will be discouraged; there will be times when you fall down. When you get discouraged in your attempts, keep in mind that you are not unique. Remember that others have gone through the same processes and they have achieved success. Success in this activity can be yours if you will put forth the necessary effort.

The fact that you have begun this course of study or have read this far in this text is evidence of your awareness of the need to discover, develop and improve your skills. You have already taken your first faltering steps. If you will apply yourself diligently to the task which you have now undertaken, the pride, the joy, and the satisfaction of being a more effective individual, a more successful communicator, and a more complete person will be the rewards which you can reasonably expect.

ACTIVITIES AND SKILL DRILLS:

1. A valuable aid in becoming a more effective speaker is to build and develop your skill in using language. During the next week start a notebook of new words which you come in contact with in your daily activities. Take time to look up the meaning, as well as the correct pronunciation, of any words you encounter. Try to use and master at least ten new words each week.

2. Select a member of the class you do not know. Conduct cross-interviews with your partner. Discover the important, the interesting, or the unusual about your partner and be prepared to tell us about him or her. Do not write out your presentation, instead, prepare an outline for this speech; include an interesting opening and closing. Give close attention to your delivery techniques but remember that you are most interested in letting us become better acquainted with the person you have interviewed.

3. Tell your audience of an interesting personal experience you have had. In this activity you may, if you prefer, substitute an imaginary or fictional event for an actual event. Tell your experience as realistically as possible and include as much detail in telling as you are able. The class will be allowed one minute to ask questions following your speech in an attempt to determine if yours is a real or an imaginary event.

CHAPTER TWO
BUILD YOUR BACKGROUND

A quality which most of us have in common is that we generally most enjoy those activities in which we excel. If you play a good game of tennis, if you are a good cook or if you excel in bridge, you generally find enjoyment in those activities. This rule applies to most skill activities, and your communication skills are no exception. The opposite is also true; we generally avoid those skills and activities in which we experience failure. Fortunately, for most people there is little difficulty encountered in avoiding those activities in which we experience limited success, but this does not hold true in our oral communications.

RECOGNIZE YOUR POTENTIAL

No matter what occupation you pursue you will be called upon to speak. Most occupations rely upon good communication, and effective speech is a necessary tool. You must decide how important speech is to *your* occupational or professional goal. Professions in sales, politics, law, and the ministry all require a heavy emphasis on public address or public speaking. Even if your plans do not call for public speaking, being an officer in a social organization, a P.T.A. member, a union representative, participating in business meetings, and making reports all require skill in effective oral communication.

Various jobs and vocations have greater or lesser demand for this ability, but unless you plan to spend your life hiding in a cave as a hermit, you are going to be called upon to communicate. Very often your chances for advancement and promotion in your chosen occupation will be directly associated with your ability to present your best image to others, and in our verbal society this image is a reflection of your ability to express yourself easily and effectively.

HAVE SOMETHING TO SAY

Our personalities are the product of our personal experiences, our associations, and our ability to react to and with our environments. Each of us is unique and special. Every experience we have ever encountered, each exposure to life, all the events we have been a part of have equipped us for our role as speakers, but we must give voice to our thoughts for them to have an effect on others.

In order to express your thoughts and ideas to others, you must first *have* thoughts and ideas. As an effective speaker, your first responsibility is to discover the nature and extent of the information that you already possess. The real test lies in your ability to communicate those ideas, experiences, and awareness to others.

Someone once asked, "If a tree falls in the forest and no one is there to hear it fall, is there truly a sound?" Another such thought might be, "Can an individual truly have an idea if he is unable to express that idea?" In speaking the thought, you set the belief. A speaker is like an artist; no matter how beautiful the picture is in the artist's mind, he can not sell it until he puts it on the canvas.

If the authors have been successful in their written communication two ideas should have been established in what you have just read . . .

1. That each of us has, by the very act of living, acquired a wealth of background knowledge which qualifies us to speak.
2. That by speaking from our existing knowledge and exercising our abilities, we can grow in knowledge and expand our ability to communicate.

ACQUIRE EXPERIENCES

Contrary to the adage, "You can't teach an old dog new tricks," you as an individual never outgrow your potential for learning. In speech situations, as in life, the best way to learn is by being introduced to new, different, and varied experiences. But here is a word of caution; just as growing old is no guarantee of maturity, exposure to new experiences is no guarantee of learning. To be successful you must become sensitive. Become aware of what goes on about you. Look and respond.

As a simple test of your sensitivity and awareness see how you rate on the following:

1. Without checking, describe the cover of the book you are now reading.
2. Is the sky cloudy or cloudless today?
3. How many steps are there in front of your home?
4. On which side of your speech instructor's head does he part his hair?

If you were unable to answer at least three of the four questions asked, you are guilty of looking but not seeing.

BECOME AWARE

To build your background as a speaker you must sharpen all of your senses. Be constantly aware of the opportunities which present themselves to you. Seek out those experiences which will enable you to add to and broaden your background. Every experience which you as a sensitive and perceptive person encounter and react to in life will add to your resources as an effective communicator.

The more you go and see and do, the greater will be your growth toward becoming a more effective communicator. The more that you respond to situations and persons in your everyday activities, the more wisdom, understanding, and sensitivity you acquire, the more successful will be your oral communications.

SEEK OUT KNOWLEDGE

If we could not profit from the knowledge and experience of others, we would never have progressed beyond the cave man in our quest for knowledge and in our search for truth. It is impossible for every person to experience every learning situation; therefore, we must learn to use the knowledge of others.

Authorities (writers, politicians, educators, and those persons or agencies to whom we can speak directly) are a valuable source of information. Included in this category are persons or groups who, because of their experience and activities, are qualified to make firsthand observations and judgements relating to their own fields. If you want information on your local police department, your local school system, or your community problems, you might well begin investigation of these matters by studying published or spoken statements or by interviewing a police department representative, a school administrator, or your city mayor.

In evaluating such information you, as the recipient, must exercise your own judgement. You must take into consideration such factors as your authority's personal qualifications, his access to available information which is pertinent and his grasp of the total situation. Other limiting factors which must be taken into consideration are his skill in successfully communicating his ideas to you and your skill and ability in accurately recording the information presented.

KNOW AND USE THE TOOLS OF LEARNING

Education has on occasion been defined as "learning to locate and to re-locate information." Of course this is a highly oversimplified definition, but it does contain a grain of truth. It would be an impossibility for you to keep in your mind, and available for immediate use, all of the facts, ideas, and information to which you are exposed in a lifetime. You must be able to locate and relocate specific information and factual data *as it is needed.*

If you are not on familiar terms with the tools and techniques of library research you are pursuing your education under an extreme handicap. Research refers to a study of those materials necessary to locating more specific information. Dictionaries, encyclopedias, card catalogs, periodical indexes, reference books, and vertical files are the general aids utilized in locating specific information.

1. Use the CARD CATALOG to learn if a library has books which will be of help to you.
2. Use the PERIODICAL INDEXES to locate current and detailed information which has appeared in regularly published sources.
3. Use ENCYCLOPEDIAS to get an overview of a topic.

4. Use DICTIONARIES to identify words, to determine correct spellings, to discover technical vocabularies, to translate unfamiliar phrases, and to learn scientific terms for common names.

5. Use REFERENCE BOOKS to find systematic surveys of an entire subject matter: year-books, specialized dictionaries, and handbooks.

6. Use VERTICAL FILES or PAMPHLET FILES to supplement your finding from books and periodicals. Often times pamphlets and clippings contain current information which can not be obtained from other sources.

In using research materials you should be aware of the strengths and weaknesses associated with these materials. A general rule applies: *those materials which are most current and up-to-date such as newspapers, periodicals and pamphlets are likely to be less accurate. Books and encyclopedias, which are generally more accurate, tend to be less current and up to date.*

In the process of acquiring your education you have likely been exposed to one or more of these general aids. In your elementary education you were introduced to the dictionary. When you became aware of the help that proper use of the dictionary could provide, you felt as if you had suddenly unlocked one of the world's great treasures. Later in your education you were probably introduced to the encyclopedia. At this point you were sure that you now had access to all of man's knowledge. If you were fortunate, at some future time you became aware of the *Reader's Guide to Periodical Literature.* Then you were certain that you could cope with any problem. Unfortunately, there are some people who never grow beyond these discoveries. For full utilization of research materials you must have some idea of the way in which they are organized.

CARD CATALOG: The card catalog is a card guide to the contents of the library. Most books have three or more entries in the catalog; a **title entry**, a **subject entry**, and an **author entry**. If you know either the author, the title of a book, or the specific subject, the card catalog will show you what is available in a particular library.

PERIODICAL INDEXES: Periodicals, materials which are published at fixed intervals of time, such as magazines, form a vital and rich source of material dealing with current thought, fact, and information. Most indexes to articles in back issues of magazines contain **subject entry** headings, which are usually very specific, and **cross references**, which suggest other sources of related information. Once you have located a specific subject heading you will discover a list of recent and current articles identified by the title of the article, the author, the title of the publication, the volume number, and the date of publication.

DICTIONARIES: A good dictionary of the English language is based upon a scientific examination of the writing and speaking habits of the users of the language; it records the origin, development, and changing use of words. The dictionary will provide you with correct spelling, pronunciations, grammar form, origin, and meaning of words you encounter and use.

ENCYCLOPEDIAS: The encyclopedia is an attempt by experts to summarize and survey all fields of knowledge. Most encyclopedias are organized around alphabetical listings of information. Indexes to the material vary with the publisher. Some indexes are contained in separate volumes, others are indexed for each volume and some have valuable cross index features. It is advisable to begin any study with an examination of the index to that particular encyclopedia.

REFERENCE COLLECTIONS: In this collection you will discover valuable sources of specific information on a variety of subjects. The effective speaker should become acquainted with the reference collections of his library. One useful aid to the location of reference materials is the *Guide to Reference Books* by Constance M. Winchell.

VERTICAL FILES AND PAMPHLET FILES: Most libraries have collections of selected up-to-date pamphlets, clippings and articles which can provide you with information on many subjects. These collections are generally maintained and organized by individual library staff members. Most collections are filed alphabetically by subject matter. If you have access to a carefully maintained, well-organized vertical file, you will often locate materials which are not available through other sources.

SUMMARY

Your one justification for standing before any group or audience is that you bring authority to the situation. Selecting worthwhile information to be communicated is, therefore, your first responsibility as a speaker.

Every experience which you have encountered in life and to which you have responded sensitively has added to your warehouse of accumulated information and knowledge. You should realize that most of man's accumulated experience and knowledge has been compiled and recorded for our use if only we possess the necessary key to unlock these treasures, and that key is *research.*

Locating facts and specific information requires that you become familiar with the special tools and aids available in your community and college libraries; the card catalog, special indexes, dictionaries, encyclopedias, reference works, and special files.

A speaker, who is well-prepared and who has something of value to share with his audience, can be reasonably sure of achieving success. Ease in speaking and self-confidence go hand in hand. The speaker who knows that he has something of value to communicate to his audience is able to concentrate his efforts on effectively presenting his thoughts and ideas to others.

ACTIVITIES AND SKILL DRILLS:

1. Visit your school library and locate the following research and reference works: Readers Guide, encyclopedias, reference collection, Atlases, current periodicals, bound volumes of periodicals, fiction, and non-fiction.

2. Check with the librarian regarding the procedures to be followed in using materials in each of the sections studied in activity one.

3. Locate and study a topic of interest to you in one of the reference works. Prepare a written report on the subject you select. Give particular attention to relating your information at your audience's language and awareness levels. Using your written report as a guide, prepare an outline and practice your presentation so that you can present a conversational discussion of your topic to your audience.

4. Using current magazines or newspapers, locate an event or topic of interest to you and your audience. After you have located as much current information as is available, use the *Reader's Guide to Periodical Literature* and locate background information on the same topic. Be prepared to give an oral presentation of the history of the problem, the current status, and probable outcome.

CHAPTER THREE
ORGANIZE YOUR THINKING

In chapter one you became aware of the importance of communication. In chapter two we discussed ways of locating information. In this chapter we shall examine a method for organizing your information. A general, a politician, a football quarterback, and you as an effective oral communicator, share a common need. The general, in directing an attack, needs carefully planned battle orders. The politician, if he hopes to be elected, needs a well thought-out campaign. The football quarterback needs many hours of work to determine his game strategy. And you, the successful speaker, will need a logical and carefully thought-out plan to be followed in preparing to speak. All meaningful activity requires careful pre-activity organization and planning if success is to be achieved.

Before meeting an audience, most effective speakers follow a definite plan in the process of getting ready to communicate. As you become more skillful as a speaker you may be able to devote less time and attention to some of these steps.

In preparing for a speech presentation you should:
1. Analyze the situation
2. Determine your objectives
3. Locate facts
4. Build a speech plan
5. Choose effective language
6. Check your readiness
7. Prepare yourself mentally and physically

Now let us carefully examine each of these steps.

ANALYZE THE SITUATION

A most important step in preparing to speak, yet one which is frequently omitted by inexperienced speakers, is to discover to whom and under what conditions your presentation is to be given. To be successful a speech must be appropriate to the *speaker,* his *audience,* and to the *occasion.*

The first step in your analysis is to determine, in so far as possible, the kind of audience you will be addressing. An analysis of your audience should seek to determine the kind of people expected, their ages, educational levels, occupations and their interests; also the language level which would be most appropriate to their background.

The second part of your analysis should be devoted to the occasion. You should attempt to determine as accurately as possible the physical and psychological conditions you are likely to meet during your presentation. An early morning breakfast meeting will present problems different from a mid-day conference or a formal dinner meeting. A group of parents gathered to discuss school problems presents a situation far removed from a group of co-workers gathered to discuss a production problem. Factors such as time restrictions, seating arrangements, physical facilities, and the audience's reasons for having gathered must all be considered in helping you decide upon the topic to be discussed and the approach which you will take towards it.

A final consideration in your analysis must be your personal interest in the subject. Before you can hope to stimulate or create an interest in other people you must first possess a sincere interest yourself. Unless you have an existing interest in your subject or a deep curiosity about the subject, it is not likely that you will enjoy doing the background work necessary to become an authority on your subject.

DETERMINE YOUR PURPOSE

Once you have selected your broad topic based upon your analysis of the audience, the occasion, and your own personal interest, you should decide upon the purpose which you intend to achieve. You should attempt in a single declarative sentence to state your purpose. Your statement should include three parts: (1) *your aim or goal,* (2) *your general topic,* and (3) *the divisions of the topic to be discussed.*

In determining the *aim or goal* of your presentation, if you are primarily concerned with increasing your audience's knowledge or information, your goal is TO INFORM.

If you seek to change or modify existing beliefs or attitudes your goal is TO PERSUADE.

On some occasions you may aim only at providing pleasure or relaxation, in which case your speech aim would be TO ENTERTAIN.

As a general rule for speeches TO INFORM, you will use a TOPICAL breakdown of the subject matter. This means you will include *selected parts of the total topic.* An example of this might be:

> *To inform* (your aim or goal) the audience about *Water Polution* (the general topic); *natural causes, man made causes, corrective efforts.* (3-5 divisions of the topic).

In Speeches TO PERSUADE the LOGICAL breakdown is generally preferred. In this pattern you insert the words 'since', 'for', or 'because' after your broad topic and provide *reasons for belief or action* as your divisions. Tell your audience *why* they should believe as you do.

For example:

> *To persuade* (aim or goal) the audience *that we should withdraw our forces from NATO* (the general topic) since, for, or because *Western Europe is economically able, the cost to the United States is prohibitive, and the threat of aggression no longer exists.* (3-5 divisions).

In arriving at a decision as to how much or how little of your topic to present, several factors must be considered. As a general rule you should use three to five divisions in covering your topic. If you have fewer than three divisions, it is likely that you will fail to cover the topic adequately. If you have more than five divisions, you risk the danger of having your audience forget the main points you want to stress. Your time limits, the audience's existing background and interest in your topic and the occasion for your speaking must all be given careful consideration in selecting and narrowing your topic to workable limits. *It is better to cover a restricted portion of your subject in detail rather than doing an inadequate job because you have attempted to accomplish too much.*

LOCATE FACTS

Once you have carefully established and stated, in thesis form, your statement of purpose, you are ready to begin gathering the *specific* information and content for your speech. In the last chapter we discussed techniques and procedures for research and library use. At this point let us examine some other means of gaining necessary content for your speech.

A source which is often overlooked is the speaker's own experiences, observations, and thinking. Your first-hand observation of events or personal happenings may have more interest for your audience than those you locate in books or magazines.

Your personal ideas and opinions, if intelligently and sincerely held, should not be overlooked. If you have no experiences or personal knowledge of your chosen topic, you may choose to seek out experiences which will be helpful. If your topic is such that reputable authorities are available to you, personal contacts and interviews are effective means of gathering information for your speeches. With the tremendous growth of mass communications (radio, television, and movies) you have yet another readily available source of information.

The important thing to remember is that material for speeches exists all around you. Informal "bull sessions" with your friends over a coffee cup, assigned areas of study in your other classes, special interests in a hobby or job provide you with valuable sources of information. The secret is in being sensitive. If you will but learn to look and see, to hear and respond, and to read extensively and be aware, there will never be a shortage of information available to you as an effective speaker.

BUILD A SPEECH PLAN

In steps one, two, and three of your preparation you have been gaining background. These steps are sometimes called "remote" preparation because they precede, or go on in advance of, the actual business of preparing immediately to speak. Starting with step four, you are actively and directly working with the speech itself.

Have you ever taken an extended trip without planning your route and destination? If you have, you may have been happy with the trip, but more likely you stayed in some less than desirable spots, wasting time and often finding yourself on dead-end roads. In giving speeches, as in taking trips, a road map is invaluable. The map is to the trip what your outline is to your speech. Just as a road map is not a trip so the outline is not intended to be the speech. Each serves only as a guide. A proper speech plan or outline is your best insurance that your speech will turn out as you would like it to.

Stated in its simplest form, in a speech you should plan on accomplishing three things: (1) *tell your audience what you plan on telling them,* (2) *tell them about your topic,* and (3) *tell them what you have told them.* These goals are sometimes referred to as PREVIEW, VIEW, and REVIEW.

In speaking, as in most other planned activities, there should be a carefully thought out beginning, middle, and end. In speeches these are generally called the INTRODUCTION, the BODY (or DISCUSSION), and the CONCLUSION.

THE INTRODUCTION In most situations you should assume that your audience is going to require a period of getting-ready-to-listen time. For this reason most successful speakers will take a few moments at the beginning of their speeches to insure that the audience is ready to listen. By planning your opening statements carefully you gain your audience's attention before you get to the most important parts of your speech. In the **Introduction**, then, you should plan first to gain the audience's attention, establish a reason for your audience to listen or create a need for them to know the information, and establish your own personal authority. After you have captured your audience's attention you should clearly state your purpose. Most of us are more comfortable when we know what is going to happen, and the same applies to a speech situation. When the audience knows where you are heading and what to expect they can give their complete attention to your discussion of the main ideas.

THE BODY In the **body** of the speech you develop, support, and elaborate upon each of the 3 to 5 major divisions of your topic. After you have arranged the main points in their most logical and effective order, you must present the facts and information necessary for full and complete discussion of these points. Under each major heading you must provide sufficient fact and information to verify, clarify, and develop each major division of your speech. Your outline serves as a source paper. It should be interesting, authorative, thorough, and *complete*. Any fact, information, content, or detail which you plan on covering in the speech should be included in the outline.

THE CONCLUSION   Once you have thoroughly discussed the main ideas in the Body, you should plan on reviewing and showing the significance of the thoughts or ideas that you have presented to your audience. This is done in your **conclusion**. In the Conclusion you have your last opportunity to drive home the ideas that you are trying to make important to your audience. In a *summary* you should plan on re-establishing the main ideas of your speech so that your audience can better appreciate and understand the relationship between the divisions of the speech as you presented them. The *last thought* or idea that you present is likely to be what your audience remembers the longest. For this reason, good speakers carefully think out their closing or final thought. Your final statement should be short and should leave your audience with something important to think about.

USE EFFECTIVE LANGUAGE

Your outline serves as a guide to effective *selection* and *arrangement* of the ideas you plan to discuss with your audience. In order to insure that you will be able to talk about these ideas easily and effectively you must at this point give careful attention to the oral expression of your thoughts and ideas. Your word choices are a most important part of your preparation. Words can affect an audience in two ways: intellectually and emotionally. You should be careful in selecting the exact word to express the exact thought that you are attempting to communicate. If there are unfamiliar or uncommon words that you have located in your research that you plan on using, be sure of the correct pronunciation and usage. Carefully consider your audience in determining your choice of words. You do not want to insult your audience's intelligence by talking down to them, and you must be careful that you do not become so technical in your choice of words as to lose your audience.

Do not at this point attempt to set or memorize your speech. Become familiar with the main ideas and thoughts. Each time you go over the ideas and thoughts try to say the *same* thing using *different* words and expressions. In this manner you are expanding your ability to discuss ideas easily and conversationally and at the same time you set the *order* of your points firmly in your mind.

As you work on the wording of your presentation, you should also give careful attention to *connectives* or *transitional* phrases. An effective transition serves as a bridge between thoughts or ideas. You should give the same careful attention to the transitions as you give to the development and discussion of your ideas. Avoid the over-used transitions such as "now", "then", and "so". Work for variety and imagination in introducing each new concept or idea.

At this point you may decide to prepare a set of "note cards" or "palm notes". On small, fairly stiff cards (3 x 5 index cards are ideal) list the main points you intend to *discuss* in your presentation. Avoid the temptation to overwrite on your cards. You prepare notes to guarantee that if you forget a point the notes will enable you to continue. Don't use your notes as a crutch. They are there to help you *if* you really need help. Avoid the tendency that some people have of overusing notes needlessly.

CHECK YOUR READINESS

Once you have the order of points and some ideas for developing and discussing these points set in your mind, practice your presentation *aloud.* Just thinking about it is not enough. Stand on your feet and imagine yourself in front of your audience. Use your voice and your body to clarify and emphasize what you have to say. If you have carefully selected and researched your topic and if you have a sincere interest in your subject, you will be enthusiastic in your presentation. When you know that you have something worthwhile, meaningful, and interesting to say to your audience, you will be more animated and more effective. A speaker who is able to become totally involved in his subject will use all of his physical facilities in communicating with his audience. Your facial expressions, your stance, and your use of gestures all become part of the total communication.

At this point it is well to check your time. In class your speeches may be timed to insure that every one has an equal opportunity to practice the skills that you are acquiring. In practice there are two even more important reasons for timing your presentations. You should learn to work with time limits because in many situations you will be asked to limit your time to accommodate other presentations. Yet another reason for learning to work within time limits is to teach you to be selective in choosing the most important information and to learn to briefly and concisely say what you mean and to mean what you say. It is best to work to a time somewhat less than that allocated to you, then if you find it necessary to adjust or to modify your presentation during the speech you have left yourself with a time buffer.

PREPARE YOURSELF PHYSICALLY AND MENTALLY

If you have followed the six previously discussed steps, you should be confident that *what* you have to say is important and well-planned. Keep in mind that you have devoted more time and attention to your topic than most people in your audience. Before, during, and after your speech keep the thought firmly in your mind that *you are the authority*. Unless you are confident of your own ability and sure of your speech content, you can hardly expect your audience to have faith in you.

How you look can sometimes be as important as what you say. Give careful attention to your appearance . . . dress appropriately for the occasion. A favorite tie or dress, polished shoes, and carefully combed hair all help you to be more comfortable.

Recognize that some nervous tension before, during, and after your speech is normal and natural. Tension is your body's way of telling you that it is ready and willing to operate at peak efficiency. All good speakers have some tension or nervousness when called upon to speak; the fact that you are nervous is a sign of respect for your audience. Making your fears work for you instead of against you will come with experience.

SUMMARY

In this chapter we have briefly examined the procedure which you should follow in preparing to speak. Each step is important to your eventual success. *All* steps should be followed for *every* speech you make. Don't take short cuts.

Once again the steps to follow are:
1. *Analyze the audience and occasion.* Find out to whom, where, when, and why you are to speak.
2. *Determine your purpose.* What do you intend to accomplish with your presentation? Ask yourself how much can you cover in the allotted time.
3. *Gather your material.* Use your own knowledge of the subject. Then do necessary research to supplement your information.
4. *Prepare a speech plan.* Organize your thinking, determine balance and completeness.
5. *Word the speech.* Decide on the wording giving careful attention to the oral expression of your thoughts and ideas.
6. *Rehearse your presentation.* Learn the main ideas to be presented and practice stating them in a variety of ways.
7. *Prepare yourself mentally and physically.* An audience is quick to sense a speaker's insecurity or lack of confidence. Be thoroughly prepared and you will be successful.

ACTIVITIES AND SKILL DRILLS:

1. Locate a copy of a recent speech. Carefully study the speech. See if you can locate and identify the following items:
   a. *The attention step.* How did the speaker gain attention to his topic?
   b. *The preview.* Did the speaker tell you early in his speech what he intended to accomplish?
   c. *The discussion.* Were you able to locate the main divisions of the speaker's content?
   d. *The summary.* Did the speaker review the main points covered in his speech?
   e. *The final thought.* Did the speaker end with a strong concluding idea?

2. Assume an imaginary situation in which you might function outside of this class; a union meeting, a P.T.A. meeting, or a social group. Plan on making a proposal for a specific action to your group. Organize your presentation using the outline form presented in this chapter.

3. Come to class prepared to make and defend a statement of conviction or belief. Your classmates will be allowed a three-minute period to ask questions. You should be prepared to answer their questions and to offer support for your stand. (In this assignment you may discover the importance of adequate research prior to meeting an audience.)

4. As an aid to your understanding of correct outline procedure, carefully study the sample outline which follows.

SAMPLE OUTLINE

PURPOSE: To inform the audience of the amazing human body: the Skeleton, the Circulatory System, and the Musculature.

INTRODUCTION

I. World of Machines   *(ATTENTION STEP)*

    A. At home.

    B. At work   *(DISCUSSION OF ATTENTION STEP)*

    C. In Education

II. Amazing Human Body   *(PREVIEW: GENERAL TOPIC)*

    A. Skeleton

    B. Circulation   *(PREVIEW: AREAS OF DISCUSSION)*

    C. Muscles

BODY

I. Skeleton   *(FIRST DIVISION OF TOPIC)*

    A. Skull   *(SUB-AREA OF FIRST DIVISION)*

       1. Flat Bones

       2. Gives features   *(DETAILS AND ELABORATION)*

       3. Protects brain

    B. Backbone   *(SUB-AREA OF FIRST DIVISION)*

       1. Irregular bones

       2. Keeps body erect   *(DETAILS AND ELABORATION)*

       3. Protects spinal cord

    C. Extremities   *(SUB-AREA OF FIRST DIVISION)*

       1. Long and short bones

       2. Contributes to motion   *(DETAILS AND ELABORATION)*

       3. Maintains balance

II. Circulatory system   *(SECOND MAIN DIVISION OF TOPIC)*

    A. Heart   *(SUB-AREA OF SECOND DIVISION)*

       1. Pumps blood

                       (DETAILS AND ELABORATION)

       2. Circulates

    B. Arteries   *(SUB-AREA OF SECOND DIVISION)*

       1. Hollow tubes

                     (DETAILS AND ELABORATION)

       2. Carries blood from heart

C. Veins   *(SUB-AREA OF SECOND DIVISION)*

   1. Collapsible tubes

                    (DETAILS AND ELABORATION)
   2. Carries blood to heart

III. Muscles   *(THIRD MAIN DIVISION OF TOPIC)*

  A. Striated   *(SUB-AREA OF THIRD DIVISION)*

   1. Under conscious control

   2. Rapid movements   *(DETAILS AND ELABORATION)*

   3. Produces motion

  B. Smooth   *(SUB-AREA OF THIRD DIVISION)*

   1. Not conscious

   2. Contracts slowly   *(DETAILS AND ELABORATION)*

   3. Changes shape of internal organs

CONCLUSION

I. Human Body   *(REVIEW: GENERAL TOPIC)*

  A. Skeleton

  B. Circulation   *(REVIEW AREAS DISCUSSED)*

  C. Muscles

II. Body wonderful machine   *(FINAL THOUGHT)*

  A. Lasts a lifetime

               (ELABORATION OF FINAL THOUGHT)
  B. Don't abuse it

BIBLIOGRAPHY:
1. Crouch, James E., *Introduction to Human Anatomy*, The National Press, California, 1964.
2. Kimber, Diana and Caroline Stackpole, *Textbook of Anatomy and Physiology*, The MacMillan Company, New York, 1955.

OUTLINE REVIEW

You will want to make note of certain areas covered.

1. At the top of the paper you state, in sentence form, your *speech purpose*. This will enable you to be sure that you know where you are going and that you will not lose direction while preparing the outline.

2. The three large divisions of the outline are identified with the headings INTRODUCTION, BODY, and CONCLUSION. Since you plan on doing certain special things in each of these sections, identify the parts of each section with Roman numerals. In the **INTRODUCTION**, the first thing you plan to do is to gain attention. Call this I. Information used to elaborate upon your attention step is labelled with capital letters (A.B.C.). At point II in your Introduction insert the 'broad topic'. This is your preview. It is at this point that you *tell* your audience the subject of your speech. Under this heading list the 'main divisions' of your speech, labelling each with capital letters (A.B.C.).

3. When you come to the BODY you are ready to discuss *in detail* the points previewed. The first division of the topic in the Body is identified with I, the second is II and the third III. Under each of these divisions list the facts, information, and details that you plan to discuss in your speech. A, B and C identify the major areas of discussion under each major division of your topic. If you want to include additional facts, details, or clarification to these points, you then make use of the notations 1, 2, and 3. As a safe rule of thumb, each main point should be developed at least to the sub-notations (1, 2, and 3).

4. In the **CONCLUSION**, as in the Introduction, you will be doing two things. First you will review the major points discussed in your speech. This is identified by the notation I as the general topic and A, B, and C as the major divisions discussed. Your final thought, which is the second point covered in the conclusion, is identified with the notation II.

CHAPTER FOUR
DEVELOP YOUR THOUGHTS

A diamond, when it is dug from the ground, looks about as pretty as any other rock which you might pick up in your own back yard. In order for the beauty and brilliance of the diamond to be shown, a trained craftsman spends many hours studying, cutting, and polishing the gem. In the hands of a trained diamond cutter it becomes a thing of great value and beauty. If it were left in the hands of an untrained person, the diamond could very easily be destroyed. The same thing can be said of a speech topic. If you know what you are doing, any topic can be made interesting and enjoyable but, without knowledge and skill in handling your material, the best of topics can become dull and uninteresting. In this chapter we will discuss the techniques and procedures for cutting and polishing your topic into a thing of beauty.

DETERMINE A LOGICAL ORDER

In preparing a speech one of your first steps is to decide upon the 'thesis' or the statement of purpose. You establish your general aim or goal (to inform, persuade, or entertain), you select your general topic, and then you decide upon the 3 to 5 divisions of your topic to be discussed. Let us now turn to a discussion of the arrangement of those divisions.

In the last chapter you were given a sample outline using the human body as the general topic. We will use that topic to illustrate the many ways you could approach this subject.

Speeches may be arranged in any of the following orders: TIME, SPACE, SEQUENTIAL, or RELATIONAL.

TIME ORDER   In using TIME ORDER the speaker is concerned with a progression of events in time. A discussion of the human body might arrange the changes and development of the body (1) from conception, (2) during childhood, (3) through adolescense,

(4) in old age. This arrangement of material shows the events in a *chronological or time sequence.*

This same order could be used to describe events as past, present, and future or to show a time sequence such as 1950, 1960, and 1970.

SPACE ORDER   When we speak of SPACE ORDER we are concerned with an arrangment of divisions based upon *location* or *position.* The sample outline made use of this type of order when it discussed the human body: (1) the skeleton, (2) the circulatory system, (3) musculature. In this order we moved from the inside of the body outward. We could have moved from top to bottom: (1) the head, (2) the chest, (3) the stomach, (4) the extremities; or we could have reversed the procedure and worked from the bottom to the top. This order might lend itself to a discussion of a rattlesnake, starting from the rattles and moving up through the snake and ending with the poisonous fangs.

SEQUENTIAL ORDER   When we arrange the divisions of the topic based upon the *continuity of events* we are using the SEQUENTIAL ORDER. Using the topic of the human body we might discuss the various parts by following an imaginary drop of blood through the body, (1) from the heart, (2) out the arteries, (3) through the system, and (4) back through the veins. This order is also called the "string of beads" order because each of the divisions of thought is tied to the next by a common quality. If you wanted to inform your audience of the major cities in the United States you might use the sequential order. You could use an imaginary trip as the 'string' or common quality, and the cities you plan to describe would be the stops along the way.

RELATIONAL ORDER   For certain topics and discussion of some subjects we make use of RELATIONAL ORDERS. In this category we find the *cause-effect* and *problem-solution* speeches. For this type of speech we arrange the points to (1) establish background, (2) present a problem, (3) offer possible solutions, and (4) justify the acceptance of one solution.

Another alternative is to reverse the process and (1) examine current happenings, (2) project future activity, and (3) suggest a course of action. Using the human body once again we might discuss a problem such as cancer in the body. The divisions of this topic might be: (1) kinds of cancer, (2) methods of detecting cancer in the body, and (3) prevention or treatment.

VERIFY YOUR THINKING

Once you have selected the divisions of your topic and arranged them in their most effective order you must then turn your attention to the development and support for each division. If you think of the main points in the outline of your speech as the skeleton, the following discussion will deal with the flesh and muscle of your presentation.

Unless you have spent many years building and establishing your reputation as an expert in a particular subject area or field, an audience expects you to provide outside authority to support your statements and assertions.

Before you can reasonably expect that your audience will accept the statements and the conclusions which you reach, you must plan on *verifying, clarifying,* and *supporting* your ideas. You do this by using various forms of verbal supporting material. The support forms include EXPLANATIONS, ILLUSTRATIONS, COMPARISONS, TESTIMONIES, and STATISTICS.

EXPLANATIONS   When we establish the *parts which make up a greater whole* we are making use of EXPLANATION. Explanations help the speaker to define and clarify ideas and concepts. They provide you and your audience with a common ground for understanding. Unless you achieve agreement on your basic terms it is unlikely that you will ever successfully achieve good communication. The following is an example of the explanation:

> "A speech outline is a device for organizing ideas for presentation to an audience. It consists of the logical divisions of the speech, it has ample detail and content, and it assures the speaker that he will have sufficient content in his presentation."

In this example we see that the "speech outline" (1) is a device for organizing ideas, (2) consists of logical divisions, (3) has ample content and detail, and (4) assures adequate content in presentation.

ILLUSTRATIONS   When we attempt to *involve the audience in a topic by painting a vivid word picture* of an event, situation, or happening we are using ILLUSTRATION. Illustrations are narrative descriptions which are told with much detail. They may be *actual* (real) events or they may be *hypothetical* (imaginary) events. Whether real or imaginary your illustrations should include names, dates, times, places, and events. When using events which have not actually happened but which could happen, you should tell your audience that the events are hypothetical. In order for your illustrations to be successful make the audience feel as if they are part of the story and have actually witnessed the events described.

"When the police arrived at the scene of the accident the first thing to meet their eyes was the young girl thrown from the vehicle. Blood covered her face and arms . . ."

Remember that you are painting a *word picture.* Choose your words carefully, involve your audience's sense of sight, sound, taste, touch, and smell in the narration.

COMPARISONS   There are two different forms of the COMPARISON. When we show the *relationship which exists between like or similar objects* we are using the LITERAL comparison. In this form we compare items of the same kind or class; schools with schools, countries with countries, or cars with cars. An example of this form of support is as follows:

"The graduation requirements at a junior college are very much like the lower division requirements of a four-year college. At the junior college you must have completed 60 or more units of work which includes a definite pattern of courses; to complete the lower division requirements at a four year college you must have completed 60 or more units of work which includes a definite pattern of courses."

When we show the *relationship which exists between dissimilar objects or between differing classes of objects* we are using the FIGURATIVE comparison. This form of support is often identified by the phrase "is like". For example:

"Student's minds are like flower gardens. They both require cultivation and attention in order to produce growth."

In this comparison we compared two entirely different kinds of things—student's minds and flower gardens. Then we showed how they could be related as being *like* one another. This is an effective form of support since it generally gives your audience an opportunity to think about common or familiar objects in a new way. This form is also used to compare unfamiliar items with items which are better known.

"A cloud *is like* a huge sponge. It absorbs moisture from its surroundings and when it is full nature wrings out the rain."

TESTIMONIES   When we use *another person's statements to support and develop our own beliefs* we are making use of TESTIMONY. Direct statements from reputable and recognized sources or quotations from another person or from literature serve to give weight and importance to your statements. For an audience to accept testimonies they must first accept the validity and authority of the source. When you quote, the audience should immediately recognize the source or you must provide them with evidence to prove the source is reputable and valid. You can establish qualification for quoted material by telling the audience about the origin and authority of the person or source quoted. For example:

"Jenkins Lloyd Jones, the editor of the Tulsa Tribune since 1941 and the recipient of the William Allen White Award from the American Society of Newspaper Editors in 1957, in a speech delivered in Chicago stated, 'Human progress has never been steady. It has washed back and forth like waves upon a beach . . . Nearly a thousand years elapsed between the fall of Western Rome and the rise of the Renaissance, and in between we had the Dark Ages in which nearly all of man's institutions were inferior to those which had gone before. "[1]

STATISTICS   When we make *use of numbers to prove a point* we are making use of STATISTICS. This support form is an effective method for giving validity and authority to the speaker's beliefs. It has rightfully been said, "Figures never lie, but liars often figure." Statistics are a valuable tool but to be effective they must be used carefully. One way a speaker establishes the validity and accuracy of his statistics is by telling the audience where the information is located. While this does not guarantee accuracy in reporting the information, it does suggest that the speaker is confident enough to provide his audience with the source of his evidence. For statistics to have the greatest influence upon your listener, there are a few simple rules to follow: (1) use rounded-off numbers instead of whole numbers (approximately 1 million is better

1. Linkugel, Wil A., R. R. Allen and Richard L. Johannesen, *Contemporary American Speeches*, Belmont California: Wadsworth Publishing Co., Inc., 1965, pp. 221-222.

than 989,762); (2) relate the numbers to your audience (1 out of 5 persons in this audience will be involved in a serious accident); and (3) either before or after presenting statistics, draw conclusions from the information presented.

"California is a land of contrasts. According to the Automobile Club of Southern California tourbook, Mount Whitney at 14,495 feet above sea level and Badwater at 279 feet below sea level represent the highest and lowest points in the United States."[1]

Advertisers and public relations experts are very much aware of the importance of using various devices and techniques in promoting their products. Advertisers sell millions of dollars worth of products each year by convincing the buyer that the product being sold is the very best. If you carefully watch television commercials or study newspaper and magazine advertisements, you will be able to locate the use of many of the support forms which we have discussed in this chapter. In locating and using verbal supporting materials a speaker should be aware of the responsibility which he assumes as an effective communicator. Through ineffective research or because of inadequate evaluation of information a speaker can often do his audience an injustice. In locating and evaluating information and evidence a speaker should attempt to be accurate, honest, and ethical. Attempt to achieve currency when locating information; locate the most recent and up-to-date information available. Be aware of biases and self-interests of your authorities; sources which have obvious prejudices or special axes to grind should be carefully evaluated. Look for consistency in your facts; even though authorities may differ on the conclusions they reach, they should be working from similar bases of information. Be cautious of generalizations; sources are often guilty of drawing broad conclusions from limited samplings. Remember that it is the speaker's responsibility, *your responsibility*, to carefully weigh and examine any evidence which you present to your audience in support of your convictions and beliefs.

---

1. American Automobile Association, *California-Nevada Tour Book, 1965-66 edition*, p. 5.

BEGINNING AND ENDING

In delivering a speech before an audience, a speaker begins with the **Introduction**, moves to the **Body** (discussion), and finishes with the **Conclusion**. However, when putting speeches together, most speakers develop the major part of their presentation, the Body of the speech, first; preparation of the Introduction and the Conclusion is then considered.

In the discussion of the outline in Chapter III, you learned that the speaker planned, in the INTRODUCTION, to (1) gain the audience's attention and (2) preview the major ideas to be discussed. The CONCLUSION was to (1) review and summarize the main concepts covered and (2) leave the audience with a strong final thought. Let us now explore these two sections of the speech in greater detail.

BEGINNING YOUR PRESENTATION   A speaker is wise to approach each opportunity to speak with the idea in his mind that he will be required to provide his audience with *a reason for listening* or with *a need to know* before he can expect their full attention. In most situations the speaker should also recognize that audiences require time to get ready for listening, and the speaker should accept that people fear the unknown. Acceptance of these principles is basic to preparing the introduction to your speech.

By previewing the broad points you wish to present to your audience, you eliminate the fear of the unknown. Getting your audience into a proper frame of mind to listen to what you have to say is more difficult. Through your *attention step,* you must establish for your audience a basis for listening. The first few minutes of your speech are crucial. As a conscientious speaker you must carefully plan your opening statements. You must stimulate your audience's interest in your topic and create a desire in their minds for the information. This is accomplished by using one or more of the following techniques for gaining and directing your audience's attention. These include the STARTLING STATEMENT, RHETORICAL QUESTION, ILLUSTRATION, QUOTATION and HUMOROUS ANECDOTE.

STARTLING STATEMENT   When you open your speech with a statement which implies or establishes a threat to your audience's life, security, or ego or when you make a statement which presents the unexpected, the unusual, or the unknown, you stimulate interest in what is to follow. A speaker can reasonably assume that he will have his audience's attention when he opens his speech with a statement such as:

> "Dating, romance, marriage, and sex usually result in children and a new state called parenthood."

The speaker's next step is to guide the audience and direct its attention through a series of steps which will show that the subject matter to be discussed is important to them and involves them directly. Once the speaker has gained the audience's attention and related the attention step to his audience, he is in a position to *preview* the topic to be discussed. A complete introduction in outline form might look like this:

I. 40,000 dead bodies   *(ATTENTION STEP)*
    A. Yearly auto deaths
    B. Could be you   *(DISCUSSION)*
    C. Someone you love
II. Automobile Safety   *(BROAD TOPIC)*
    A. The driver
    B. The vehicle   *(DIVISIONS TO BE DISCUSSED)*
    C. The road

In all of the techniques which we shall discuss, the opening statement is designed to stimulate audience interest. The elaboration of the attention step relates the topic to the audience. Unless the speaker makes his topic vital and important to and for his listener, the best that he can hope for is polite attention. Active response can only follow active involvement.

RHETORICAL QUESTION   Another effective way to begin your speech is to ask a question of your audience. Your intent, in using this type of opening, is to involve the audience by making them think with you about the subject to be explored. You do not desire nor expect direct answers to your questions, only a mental response. A speaker might begin a speech on "Campus Marriages" with the rhetorical question:

> "What do you really expect to accomplish by going to college?"

In elaboration of this attention step, the speaker provides several possible answers and, in this fashion, leads his audience to his preview as indicated in the following example.

I. Why College?   *(ATTENTION STEP)*
   A. Occupation
   B. Skills
   C. Knowledge   *(DISCUSSION)*
   D. Co-curricular activities
   E. Dating
II. Campus marriages   *(BROAD TOPIC)*
   A. Extent of
   B. Reasons for   *(DIVISIONS TO BE DISCUSSED)*
   C. Success of

ILLUSTRATION   Most everyone enjoys an interesting story. As we discussed previously, illustrations can deal with actual events or with events which, though they have not happened, could have happened. In using the story or illustration you should include sufficient detail to involve your audience through appealing to their senses of sight, sound, touch, taste, and smell. Include names, dates, times, and events. The more realistic you can make the story in the retelling, the greater the involvement of the audience. A speech on "Automobile Safety", which begins with a detailed narrative, would prepare your audience and put them in a proper frame of mind to respond to your information.

> "Tuesday, August the second began as a quiet, routine patrol for officer Ken Willard. He was on the 4:00 P.M. to midnight or grave yard shift. Before this night ended for officer Willard, the name 'graveyard shift' was to take on very special meaning. His first indication of trouble came when the call to proceed to Highway 6 . . ."

An illustration is an excellent audience-involving opening. In using this type of beginning you must rehearse your opening until you can achieve a conversational ease and effectiveness.

QUOTATIONS   A speaker must establish early in his presentation his personal authority and qualification to speak. This is one reason for using the quotation as an attention step. The speaker quickly establishes his status as a well-prepared speaker and associates himself with the experts and authorities. When using this technique to begin, as well as when using it as a form of support within the speech, the person or literary source quoted should be recognized as being an authority and should be identified for your audience. A speech on 'World Peace' might begin with the quotation opening—

> President John F. Kennedy in his 'Inaugural Address', January 20, 1961 said, "Now the trumpet summons us again — not as a call to bear arms, though arms are needed; not as a call to battle, though embattled we are; but a call to bear the burden of a long twilight struggle, year in, and year out, rejoicing in hope, patient in tribulation — a struggle against the common enemies of man; tyranny, poverty, disease and war itself."[1]

A speaker who chooses to begin his speech with a quotation has a responsibility for being accurate in selecting or cutting the material to be used. The author's intent, as established in the total presentation, should be respected. You should not change or modify the ideas expressed from the intent of the total quotation.

HUMOROUS ANECDOTE   A funny story can serve to relax tension in the speaker and in his audience, but, to be used effectively, it must do more than just entertain. When using a humorous anecdote to begin a speech, the speaker should measure the opening against the following yardsticks: (1) Is the story really funny? (2) Can I tell it effectively? and (3) Does it relate to my speech purpose? There are few experiences so disturbing to both the speaker and the audience as when this type of opening has been planned and the speaker discovers too late that he has failed to satisfy these requirements. Unless the story is amusing, related to the topic, and well-told, it should not be used. The story which follows might be used in a speech, but it also has a moral which is appropriate to this discussion of speech introductions.

> "A farmer in need of a mule heard of a neighbor who had one for sale. After seeing the mule, a deal was arranged. The man selling the mule told the new owner that the mule was a very hard worker, but he worked best if he was treated with kindness. The first morning the new owner tried to get the mule out of the barn, but the mule refused to budge. Using all of his patience he coaxed and urged the mule with only the kindest of

1. Capp, Glenn R., *Famous Speeches in American History,* Indianapolis: Bobbs–Merrill Company, Inc., 1963, p. 238.

language. In desperation he called the original owner and complained. When the seller came to his neighbor's house, he picked up a large two by four and hit the mule a resounding whack over the rump. In amazement the new owner protested, 'but you told me to use kindness.' To this the original owner replied, 'That's very true. But first you have to get his attention'."

The moral of this story can serve to summarize this entire discussion. FIRST YOU HAVE TO GET ATTENTION. Once you have your audience ready to listen, you can then get to the other important work at hand.

The PREVIEW should follow your attention step. At this point your audience should have its attention directed and focused on you and your subject. By telling the audience what is to follow, you enable them to begin thinking *with you* about your topic. Using the thesis or purpose statement which you have prepared as part of your organization, you should at this point tell the audience the general topic to be discussed and the divisions of that topic to be explored.

ENDING YOUR PRESENTATION   Following a thorough discussion of your topic in the body of your speech you are then ready to conclude your presentation. Unfortunately, many speakers make the mistake of not giving enough attention to their concluding statements. The last thing said by a speaker is likely to be what is remembered the longest. For this reason you should very carefully plan your CONCLUSION.

When small children come home from school, parents often ask, "What did you learn in school today?" Generally, the answer received is, "Nuthin'." To eliminate this response, many smart teachers end the day by telling the student what he learned that day. You can take a clue from the smart teacher. To be sure that your audience remembers what it has learned from your speech, in your conclusion *tell them what you have told them.* Your first step in the conclusion is to summarize. This may be accomplished in one of three ways: the SIMPLE SUMMARY, the PARAPHRASED SUMMARY, or the GENERAL SUMMARY.

THE SIMPLE SUMMARY   Using the points previewed in the introduction as a guide, the simple summary restates the major topic and the divisions of the topic which have been discussed. This type of summary has the advantage of building retention through repetition. Through your use of the same words to express the main ideas of your speech in the **preview, view** and **review** you are setting the ideas in your audience's minds. Advertisers often make use of this technique in selling products to the public. They repeat their message until it is retained by the buyer through use of a catchy slogan or phrase. To illustrate the effectiveness of the technique let us use two every famous slogans. "You can be sure if it's_____" and "At_____ progress is our most important product." Unless you have been hiding in a cave for many years you should be able to fill in the advertiser's name without any trouble. (*Did you fill in Westinghouse and General Electric?*)

Though the simple summary is effective, some speakers feel that it presents an overly mechanical approach. For this reason some speakers prefer a more subtle approach.

THE PARAPHRASED SUMMARY   The speaker still reviews and restates the major ideas he has covered when using the paraphrased summary. Instead of using the same words to end the speech as he used in the preview, the ideas are presented with a fresh approach. Using the same ideas, he attempts to create added interest through different words to express the same thoughts. This type of summary requires more attention but is less likely to appear mechanical.

To illustrate this type of summary, if your statement of purpose in the preview was, "To convince the audience that the Electoral College should be abolished because 1. The historical basis no longer exists, 2. Present day voters are better informed, and 3. The popular vote better reflects the will of the people," your paraphrased summary of these points in the conclusion could be stated . . . "Since the original reasons for the Electoral College no longer apply, since mass communications provide a better opportunity for the voter to know the candidates and since the Electoral College takes your right of direct expression from you, it is apparent that we must eliminate this outmoded and outdated system."

THE GENERAL SUMMARY   The least apparent, the most difficult and, perhaps, the most effective type of summary is accomplished by the general summary. In this type of summary the speaker reviews the major concepts or conclusions he has drawn from his information. Unless the speaker has become thoroughly involved with his topic and has reached the point of being authorative on the subject, he should avoid this type of conclusion. If, however, the speaker is capable of focusing his thoughts, concepts and impressions to the point where he can form valid judgements he may effectively use this technique.

In the general summary the speaker attempts to present a series of related conclusions, or courses of action, based upon his analysis and background. An example of this type of conclusion can be seen in a presidential 'State of the Union' message in which the President moves from specific factual data in the discussion to *general* conclusions or assumptions in the reviews.

Each of the summary types discussed, the simple, paraphrased, or general, serve to review and reinforce the major points developed in the body of the speech. Once the speaker has completed his review he directs his audiences attention to the final or closing statement.

The **final thought** should attempt in a few carefully chosen words to impress your audience with the central concept or message of your presentation. This is accomplished by the use of a catchy slogan, a pointed testimony, or by a suggestion for a definite course of action to be followed. It is important to remember that your closing thought must be given with finality. You must, by your voice and manner, tell the audience that you are through.

SUMMARY

In this chapter we have explored and examined various means and techniques for guiding and directing an audience's thoughts during speech presentations. We have discussed the arrangement of main ideas: **time, space, sequential** and **relational.** The forms of verbally supporting your thoughts were explained: **explanations, illustrations, comparisons, testimonies** and **statistics.** Methods for gaining your audience's attention in the introduction were illustrated: the **startling statement, rhetorical question, illustration, quotation** and **humerous anecdote.** And, finally, the methods for summarizing in the conclusion were discussed: the **simple summary,** the **paraphrased summary** and the **general summary.**

With the acquisition of knowledge and skill comes certain responsibilities. The word "ethics" comes to us from the Greek word "ethos" which means character. To the ancient Greeks, a man's moral character was his most valuable possession. As a modern day oral communicator you, too, have a moral and ethical responsibility. A speaker must be true to his audience and to himself. You must use your knowledge of technique and procedures to worthy ends. Be accurate and honest as you use your knowledge, information, and skill.

ACTIVITIES AND SKILL DRILLS:

1. Decide upon a topic or belief about which you have strong feelings. State your conviction in a single declarative sentence. Organize a speech in which you attempt *to convince* your audience that your belief is correct. Carefully study your topic and be prepared to defend your stand. The audience will be allowed to question you on your belief following your speech presentation.

2. Organize and do adequate research on a topic which you feel will be of interest to you and your audience. In this presentation plan on using all five of the Forms of Verbal Support at least once. Your aim or goal in this presentation should be *to inform*, plan to increase your audience's information and knowledge on a topic of significance. The class will, following your presentation, attempt to locate and identify each of the forms of support which you presented in your speech.

3. Carefully study one of the student outlines and speeches in the Appendix C. Keeping in mind that these were prepared by students, be prepared to give an oral critique and evaluation of their use of: (1) effective arrangement of the divisions of the speech, (2) the utilization of verbal support, (3) the Introduction, and (4) the Conclusion.

CHAPTER FIVE
PUT YOUR BEST FOOT FORWARD

There's an old saying which states "Clothes make the man." There is a good deal of truth in this statement. We often make lasting judgements of people based upon first impressions. You form opinions about your instructors, political candidates, and people you meet largely on the basis of what you see and hear.

Up to this point we have dealt mainly with techniques and procedures for preparing your speech content. In this chapter we shall discuss the ways and means for most effectively delivering your information to an audience. We shall discuss your appearance, your posture, stage fright, and vocal effectiveness.

MAKE A GOOD IMPRESSION

The first impression which you make on another person or upon an audience is primarily a visual impression. Remember your first day in speech class. As you came into the classroom you probably looked around you and began to evaluate your classmates in an attempt to "size-up" the competition. When your instructor came into the room, you very likely formed some mental judgements before he or she ever said a word. When you first meet a person you begin to judge him largely upon what meets the eye. An audience also begins to judge you as a person and a speaker from what they first see.

As a speaker you have but one reason or justification for standing before your audience. You must be, and your audience must accept you as, an authority. If you have given careful attention to proper preparation of your content you will be authorative, but, unless you look like an authority, your audience will not fully accept you in that role. Careful attention to such things as shined shoes, neat clothing and combed hair may seem trivial or unimportant, but they can do much toward influencing your listeners' reactions to you as a speaker. If you give careful attention to your dress and appearance, you increase your chances of creating a favorable first impression.

Once you have created a good impression everything which you do from that point must serve to reinforce that idea.

WATCH YOUR POSTURE   One of the most obvious clues to a speaker's confidence is his posture. To project interest and enthusiasm to an audience you must appear alert and interested. A person who walks briskly into the speaking situation looks sure and confident. Before you start speaking, it is good technique to get set both mentally and physically. If you take a moment to get comfortably balanced on both feet, arrange your thoughts, and allow the audience time to get ready to listen, you further create the proper mood. A speaker who constantly rocks and sways, shifts his weight from one hip to the other, or is in constant motion looks unsure of himself and very awkward. Poor posture is a distraction and destroys the positive image you hope to create. Later in this chapter we shall discuss movement and gestures but, before you think about these meaningful movements, you must first master the technique for standing comfortably still.

Since each person has his own skeletal and muscular characteristics, posture becomes a very individual matter. To determine your own best position, stand comfortably erect with your weight evenly balanced on both feet and both hips. Notice the position of your feet. If they are too close together or too far apart you are likely to be uncomfortable. Your heels should be slightly separated and your toes slightly pointed out. Women should avoid the typical model's stance which places one foot at right angles to the other foot. Once you have determined the comfortable placement of your feet make note of their position. This is the stance which you should assume prior to beginning your presentation.

The placement of the hands and arms also deserves some thought. Remember that what you are attempting to communicate, with your proper posture, is an image of poise and confidence. Anything which calls attention away from the message which you plan to convey should be eliminated. Placing your hands in front of or behind your body, crossing your arms, putting your hands in your pockets, or hooking your thumbs in your belt all tend to create an impression of discomfiture and tells your audience that you are ill at ease. The best place for your arms and hands is at your side. You should learn to let your arms hang naturally and comfortably to your sides. In this position, if you have notes or if you plan to use communicative gestures, your hands are free and available for use and do not create a distraction.

In most formal speaking situations you will likely be provided with a speaker's stand or a lectern. Remember that the purpose of a lectern is to hold the speaker's notes; it is not intended to hold the speaker. Even when standing behind a lectern, you should be conscious of proper posture. Don't lean, rest, or hang over the lectern. If you are using notes, which you place on the lectern, it is permissable and proper to lightly rest your hands on the top of the lectern.

As important as good posture is to the speaker, it is but one element of speaker poise. Learning about stage fright and methods for reducing your fears will contribute to your poise and authority.

CONTROL YOUR FEARS

Every person of normal or above average intelligence knows and experiences the emotion known as fear. As with most of our emotions it is designed to serve a vital and necessary function in our lives. For our caveman ancestors, fear was necessary for survival. When Og slouched out of his cave and met a sabertoothed tiger waiting for him he experienced fear. His fear produced many life-saving internal organic changes. His glands pumped their juices into his system, his senses were sharpened, and his body got ready to fight or to run. Though we have come a long way over the centuries and our lives are very much safer than in Og's time, there is still a little bit of Og in each of us. Our bodies still prepare themselves in much the same way when we encounter strange or fearful situations.

Standing before an audience is a fear producing occasion. We fear the audience's reactions to us and to our ideas, we fear that we may forget words or thoughts or we fear that we may not live up to our own or our audience's expectations of us. Though the cause of our fear may be different, our reactions to the fear are the same as our caveman ancestors. Our body prepares itself to fight or to run . . . and we know that we can do neither. The situation is comparable to racing the engine on an automobile, letting out the clutch, and then holding on the brakes. If you were to try this on your car, it would shake and strain; if the brake were not released, the car would soon stall. The same thing can happen to you as a speaker. Your body is running at high speed and you are mentally holding on the brakes. Is it any wonder that you have some reactions?

Now that you better understand the cause of your shaking hands, trembling knees, perspiring palms and the butterflies in your stomach, let us turn our attention to some methods for coping with your stage fright.

An important first step in controlling *stage fright* is to accept it as normal and natural. You are not alone or unique in your feelings. Everyone who appears before an audience experiences some nervous tension before, during, and after his performance. Even people who spend much of their lives before audiences (comedians, singers, sportsmen, politicians, and teachers) have fear and tension. With experience and practice they have learned to reduce and control their fears, and so can you. A common cause of fear in beginning speakers is lack of sufficient or effective preparation. If the speaker is not prepared then he deserves to be nervous. If you have a worthwhile topic, have spent your time prior to your speech presentation in becoming an authority, and have prepared your materials in an effective manner, you will have taken effective measures towards controlling excessive or unnecessary fear and tension.

As a second step toward controlling your fears, realize that the tension which you feel is both good and helpful. Tension is your body's way of telling you that it is operating at a peak performance level. Your body and your mind are ready to operate at their most efficient level under tension; your heart beat quickens to provide additional blood to the brain and to your muscles, functions unnecessary to survival action such as digestion are slowed down, and adrenilin and other body fluids enter the blood stream to provide needed stimulation. Your body is readied for maximum effort because of the tension.

By understanding and accepting your fear you will have taken an important psychological step toward the reduction of the negative aspects of stage fright. Knowing what is happening and why it happens should enable you to accept the tension which you possess as normal and necessary.

If you make use of meaningful and planned **movement** and **gesture**, you can further reduce the ill effects of your tension. A movement forward, back or to one side signals a change of thought in your presentation. A definite movement to a new position allows you an opportunity to release the brake and to make use of your muscles. The use of your hands, arms, or facial muscles to enhance your communication further serves to relax your body. When you move, do so meaningfully and consciously. Avoid nervous pacing or rocking. Do not fidget with your notes or your clothing. Once you have signaled a change in thought by your movement then assume your authorative poised posture again.

When using your hands to **gesture**, a few simple suggestions will enable you to get the most out of the movement. Gestures which can not be seen do little to aid communication. When you gesture be sure that your hands are above your waist. Move your elbows away from your sides to allow your gestures freedom of movement. Gestures should normally start from the center of the body and move away from the body in curved rather than in straight lines. Do not plan specific gestures for use at specific places in your speech; overly-rehearsed gestures lose their effectiveness. During your rehearsal, if you feel the urge to use your hands to aid communication, by all means do so; then in your speech, if you feel the desire to reinforce your words with movement or gesture, they should be allowed to happen. *First must come the feeling, then can come the action.*

Another technique which has proven successful for many speakers is to consciously relax your body before your speech presentation by **controlled breathing**. If you will take several deep breaths of air into your lungs and slowly allow the air to escape, you do two things. First, you provide your body with additional oxygen and, secondly, by the slow, controlled exhalation of the air, you force your upper body muscles to relax.

The suggestions which have been discussed are all aimed at treatment of the symptoms of stage fright. As in medicine, this is a direct course of action often taken. A better method of treating a physical ill is to work on the cause of the complaint. Your efforts to study about oral communication has begun the work on a cure for the *real* cause of your problem. The very best remedy which anyone can offer you for reducing your fear and tension is to speak, speak, and to speak. Exposure to speech situations and frequent practice before audiences is the best way to lose your fear. Once you have become aware of your strengths as a speaker and discover the satisfaction which comes to you in having done a good job as an oral communicator, you will find that your fears in speaking before any audience will be greatly reduced.

As in most other activities, you must have the correct tools to do a good job and you must know how to use those tools properly. One of the speaker's most important tools is his voice. Assuming that each of you has the necessary physical apparatus for producing speech, let us now turn our attention to the techniques for using that tool most effectively.

DEVELOP VOCAL EFFECTIVENESS

If you were to count the number of words which you spoke and listened to in just one day, the number would likely stagger your imagination. And, if you were to listen very carefully, you would probably be much more surprised to find how few good voices you would hear. As with most of the qualities that relate to good speech, your vocal effectiveness can be increased with conscious effort on your part. The three areas of concern which we shall examine are **voice production, articulation,** and **vocal variety**.

VOICE PRODUCTION   Any discussion of voice must begin with some basic understandings about the production of vocal sound. You may be surprised to learn that your voice begins in your stomach. This is a slight exaggeration; the location is accurate but the organ is not. The motor or power source for your voice is the *diaphragm.* This is a muscle which separates your chest cavity from your stomach area. The normal operation of the diaphragm provides you with a controlled and sustained source of vital air. As the diaphragm expands it causes air to be pulled into the lungs; as the diaphragm contracts it pushes the air out of the lungs. If you watch a baby cry or observe a dog after it has run hard, you will notice that it is the stomach area which goes in and out with each breath. As the air is pushed out of the lungs it then passes over the *vocal folds* (also called the vocal cords); this is another set of muscles in the throat which can be tightened or relaxed to produce varying sounds. If you have ever blown air into a balloon and then stretched the neck of the balloon together to make a noise, you can visualize the operation of the vocal folds. As the muscles are pulled tighter you make high sounds; as the muscles are relaxed you produce lower tones.

The sounds produced by the vocal fold operation then passes through your throat and into your head. Just as a piano, a guitar, or a violin requires a *sounding box* to improve and amplify the sounds, the sounds you produce require this same action. As the sound bounces back and forth and around the cavities in your head it develops individual qualities and overtones, but it is still only noise at this point. To change this noise into recognizable speech requires the use of the *articulators.* You use your lips, tongue, teeth, jaw, and palate (roof of the mouth) to form, shape, mold, and create recognizable sounds and words.

This is a very much simplified and brief description of the very complicated process of speech production. It is vital that you understand the development of the sounds if you are to work for improvement of faulty habits. A common fault associated with poor vocal control is poor or improper breathing. If an audience is to be influenced by your words and ideas, they must first be able to hear you. Improper *breath control* can cause you to run out of breath in the middle of a thought, or it can be the reason why people are unable to hear you easily when you speak. As we have seen, the diaphragm is the motor for your voice. It is an automatic muscle which means that it operates without any conscious effort on your part, but, as with any other muscle in your body, it can be strengthened, and, through exercise, you can develop more conscious control of it. You should learn to control *inhalation* and *exhalation;* two simple exercises can help you to achieve this control. First, to develop controlled inhalation, stand erect and place your hand on your stomach. Open your mouth slightly and take in a short gasp of air. As you inhale quickly, you should feel your stomach move outward. Through practice you should learn to cause the diaphragm to expand with only a short, quick intake of air through the mouth. This is the way you should replenish your air supply while speaking. While mastering this technique you should practice controlled exhalation. You want to learn to provide a continuous flow of air behind your words. This control is obtained through the slow tightening of the diaphragm. To develop this control lay down on the floor and place a book on your stomach. Practice raising the book as high as possible with a short gasp and then allow the air to slowly escape from your mouth. As the diaphragm contracts, the book should slowly sink. Just a few minutes spent each day on these exercises will increase your control of the air supply necessary to effective speech.

Once you have developed a controlled air supply you should direct your attention to verbal clarity.

ARTICULATION   The articulators: lips, tongue, teeth, jaw, and palate, mold and shape the sounds into words. Articulation is primarily a matter of good or poor habits. If you have developed sloppy habits over the years that you have been speaking, your first step to better articulation is awareness. Some of the more common articulation errors are *lazy lips, tense jaws,* and *improper placement of the tongue.*. Speakers who consistently say "jist" instead of "just", "git" for "get", "fur" in place of "for", "kin" when they mean "can", or "becuz" rather than "because" are guilty of sloppy or lazy articulation. To properly form these words and sounds requires full and active articulation. Exercises such as opening the jaw as wide as possible, wagging the jaw back and forth, and puckering the lips all serve to develop more flexibility in the use of the articulators. Another less common articulation flaw is the foreign language shift. Faulty pronunciation of "v" or "w" sounds in a person of Germanic background or the "r"-"l" shift in the Japanese requires the attention of a trained speech correctionist.

Most common articulation errors are subject to improvement based upon close attention by the speaker. As you become more aware of the influence which proper articulation has upon your listener you should work for *cleaner, clearer,* and *more precise* articulation.

Assuming your awareness of the importance of proper vocal production and articulation, let us now turn to another most important aspect of voice, your vocal flexibility.

VOCAL VARIETY   A voice without variety is like a stew without seasoning. The stew may contain nourishing ingredients but it just wouldn't taste very good. You may present interesting ideas to your audience but you can not hope to achieve interest or enthusiasm without variety. **Vocal variety** is achieved by regulating the four variables of your voice: **rate, pitch, force,** and **pause.**

Variety in **rate** is achieved by speaking slowly or more rapidly. As a good rule of thumb, exciting, active events require a more rapid rate. Solemn or serious events demand a slower over-all rate. The secret for successful variety of any sort is to avoid being regular and constant in the use of any of the vocal variables.

Pitch refers to the basic tonal quality of the speaker. Once again the key is flexibility. Keep in mind that the low, rich tones are the most pleasing to the ear. You should work to cultivate and develop the more pleasing low-range of your tonal qualities.

Force means volume, loud and soft. An effective way to stimulate interest is by a shift in force. Even when you reduce your force, you must never fail to speak with sufficient force to be easily heard. You create variety in force in two ways—mentally and physically. Physically, you must work to supply sufficient air behind each word. Mentally, if you think of your voice as moving up and out of your body, you will provide the necessary internal stimulus.

Pause is the lack of sound. This final variable is often over-looked by inexperienced speakers . . . Through effective use of the pause you can emphasize words, build interest to key thoughts, and stress important ideas. If you have an opportunity to listen to an effective speaker or to your favorite comedian, notice how much his communication is influenced by the use of dramatic and planned pause. A pause, coupled with inflection, further serves to provide *verbal punctuation*. A brief pause sets off units of thought within a sentence and longer pauses signal the end of a completed idea. *Inflection*, the upward or downward shifts in pitch, also serves to identify punctuation, an *up* inflection generally suggests a question mark, a *down* inflection indicates a period, while a pause with no shift in inflection generally means the same as a comma in writing.

A voice which lacks variety in **rate, pitch, force** and/or **pause** is dull, flat, and uninteresting. To achieve success as a speaker, you must be aware of the effect your voice has on an audience. Your voice is like a fine instrument, but to get the best use of it you must learn to play it. It is like having a concert grand piano in your living room, you can either settle for playing "Chopsticks" on it or you can, with practice, learn to make beautiful music with it.

SUMMARY

In this chapter we have explored the techniques of good delivery. You make your first impression on an audience before you say your first word so you should give careful attention to your appearance. **Posture** is a clue to your poise and authority; good posture and balance serves to assure your audience of your self confidence. **Stage fright** is good and beneficial; it is a normal and natural part of appearing in public. You must learn to control your fears, but you should not expect to lose all of your tensions. An **interesting voice** is dependent upon several factors. First, you must develop a controlled air supply since proper breath control is essential. **Articulation** is necessary in shaping and forming clear and recognizable speech. **Vocal variety** is the spice in the soup, changes in rate, pitch, force, and pause add interest and meaning to your speech presentation.

Good delivery is important to success as a speaker, but you must never forget that delivery is not an end in itself. To be a good speaker and oral communicator you must first have something worthwhile to say, you must organize your content in a logical and effective manner and, finally, you must learn to deliver your thoughts and ideas skillfully, effectively, and well.

ACTIVITIES AND SKILL DRILLS:

1. Pantomime is the art of telling a story or describing an event without the use of speech. Without using any props other than a chair, tell your audience a story. There should be a series of events which occur that leads up to the climax or major happening in your story. Realize that your posture, facial expressions, and hand movements all contribute to the success of your pantomime.

2. Plan to demonstrate to your audience how something is made, done, functions or operates. Research and outline your topic. Locate and bring to class all of the necessary materials to be used in your speech.

3. Illustrations or stories are often used in speeches as an Introduction, in the Body, or in the Conclusion. Locate a short story which you think will be of interest to your audience. (*i.e.*, a Thurber fable) Study the selection carefully and locate the main events which occur. Practice re-telling the story in your own words. Come to class prepared to tell the story giving careful attention to your articulation and the use of **vocal variety** to create interest.

CHAPTER SIX
SPEAK TO THE OCCASION

Walter Mitty is a famous character in literature. In the short story "The Secret Life of Walter Mitty", we are able to observe the main character indulging in his favorite past time . . . daydreaming. Any psychology student can tell you that a little daydreaming is good for anyone, but, eventually, a mature person comes to the realization that to accomplish anything worthwhile you must set goals and work to achieve them.

In this chapter we shall discuss some of the specialized uses of your communication skills. As with any skill that we acquire and develop, it is of no value unless we put it to work. Walter Mitty was able to be a success only in his dreams, you can achieve success by putting your knowledge to work for you.

In your school activities, social organizations, or on your job, you will have many opportunities and occasions for MAKING REPORTS, TAKING PART IN DISCUSSIONS, and FUNCTIONING IN MEETINGS. Each of these oral communication activities requires special skills and techniques.

MAKING ORAL REPORTS

Each of us has and makes use of a number of different vocabularies. We have a speaking vocabulary, a writing vocabulary, and a comprehensive vocabulary. Each of these is dependent upon your past experiences with and exposure to books, education, and people. The average student's speaking vocabulary is more limited than his writing vocabulary and both of these are less than his comprehensive vocabulary. You know and can recognize many more words than you normally use. In preparing oral reports you have two special communication problems: (1) you must learn to write to your audience's level of understanding, and (2) you must write for the ear not for the eye. If you have ever been called upon to read aloud a composition you wrote, you are probably aware that a well-written report does not necessarily make a good oral report.

In preparation for an oral report or a presentation which is to be read aloud, you should follow the seven steps in organization (review Chapter III), but you must add two additional steps: PREPARATION OF THE MANUSCRIPT, and MANUSCRIPT MARKINGS.

PREPARATION OF THE MANUSCRIPT   After you have "analyzed your audience and occasion," "determined your purpose," "gathered your materials," and "prepared your outline," you are ready to "word your speech." In the oral report, at this point, you must determine the *exact* language and the precise wording of your speech. Using your outline as a guide, talk the speech through several times, getting the feel of the words. Once you have achieved a conversational quality, write out the entire speech in **manuscript form.**

The main difference between writing for the eye, a composition, and writing for the ear, a manuscript, is that a reader can re-read what is in your composition, but a listener must receive the information from a single exposure. If the listener misses a thought or idea he cannot go back. You must do all that you can to insure that he does not miss anything that you want him to remember. To achieve effective communication you should plan internal *previews* and *summaries;* let them know what is to be covered and what has been said. Give careful thought to **transitions:** discussion leading from one thought or idea to the next. Keep your sentence structure simple; avoid complex sentences with many subordinate clauses.

Choose your words carefully and write to your audience's level of understanding. As you continue to be exposed to influences beyond your immediate family, friends, neighbors and other adults, you should become aware of the many different levels of *language use* which exists. With maturity you should begin to recognize that special situations call for special differences in the use of words. Speech patterns appropriate to one situation or occasion may be totally inappropriate for another. The language you use in college classrooms might not be at all acceptable on your job or at home. If the other members of your family or friends are not attending college and you used your collegiate vocabulary with them, they might think that you were showing off. By the same reasoning, the vocabulary which you use on your job might not necessarily be the one you should use in your college classes. The trick is to learn which of your vocabularies is most appropriate for the situation.

Once you have settled on the language, very clearly write or type a clean copy of your manuscript. In preparing your final copy leave a space between each line (double-space) so that during your speech you will be able occasionally, to look away from your manuscript, to look at your audience and then back to the next word or idea. Another reason for the spaces between the line is to allow room for the manuscript markings and last minute corrections or additions.

MANUSCRIPT MARKING   Someone once defined a college lecture as a means of transferring the instructor's notes to the students' notes without having the information go through the minds of either the student or the instructor.

Since the speaker decides upon the exact wording of his speech in the manuscript, poor speakers often fail to allow for the ideas going *through* their heads while speaking. The result of this type of delivery is frequently a voice that is dull, flat, and regular and a speech which fails to accomplish its purpose. Another common fault in reading from the manuscript is inappropriate or improper phrasing which results in loss of meaning. **Marking your manuscript** can help you to avoid these common errors.

Using the clean copy of your report, read your material aloud. Listen carefully and note where you make use of meaningful and conversational pauses. At each of these places put a slash (/) mark. (In using these and other markings to be discussed, it is advisable to use pencil so that you can make changes if you change your mind about the placement of the markings). At the end of each completed thought, or where you plan a longer pause, put a double slash (//). *Normal punctuation is necessary to proper meaning; it is an eye signal.* In preparing your manuscript to be read aloud you may find it useful to make use of additional punctuation; dashes (- - -) to separate thoughts, or dots (. . .) to indicate portions of ideas or as signals for more meaningful pauses.

Once you have decided upon the groupings of words into meaningful segments of thought, you should look for *key words* to receive special emphasis within each thought unit. *Underline important words which you plan to stress.* To insure adequate and effective vocal variety you may mark places where you plan upward inflections ($\mathcal{A}$) or downward inflections ($\curvearrowright$). If you determine that certain words or thought units are to be given together with others these are marked with the bridge ($\frown$).

Patrick Henry's famous "Give me liberty, or give me death" speech, which he delivered in the Virginia House of Burgesses on March 23, 1775, might look like this if it were marked for reading aloud:

"It is in vain sir, / to continue the matter //. Gentlemen may cry Peace, Peace, // but / there is no peace.// The war is actually begun //? The next gale / that sweeps from the north / will bring to our ears / the clash of resounding arms //! Our brethren / are already in the field! // Why stand we here idle //? What is it that gentlemen wish? Is life so dear / , or peace so sweet, / as to be purchased / at the price of chains and slavery //?

Forbid it, / Almighty God //! I know not / what course / others may take; // but for me, // give me liberty or give me death!//

You should realize that speech patterns and phrasing are individual matters and will differ from one speaker to the next. There is no one correct way to deliver a speech. Try reading Patrick Henry's speech aloud to see if you agree with the markings. If you do not agree with the authors' markings you may want to try remarking the passage to see if you can prepare it more effectively. You should notice in the selection the excellent word choices and the precise sentence structure.

TAKING PART IN DISCUSSIONS

In a democracy, decisions are often made on the basis of the cooperative efforts of large and small groups. Learning to be an effective participant in group decision-making will enable you to receive the full benefits and rewards of active citizenship.

In this section we will discuss the most basic kind of **group discussion,** the BUZZ SESSION, as well as the more formal structure of the SYMPOSIUM and the ROUND TABLE format.

BUZZ SESSIONS   The most common, and the least formal kind of the discussion is the BUZZ SESSION. This is a means by which people can explore, examine, accept, or reject possible courses of action and exchange ideas and opinions cooperatively.

As in all discussions some basic requirements must be met if success is to be achieved. The first essential *is order*; this does not mean formality, but courtesy and consideration of others must be observed. Second, there must be some *general interest or item of mutual concern.* Third, there must be an *attitude of cooperation;* compromise and adjustment of ideas must be expected. Finally, a *general goal or purpose* must be established to prevent needless and unnecessary tangent discussion.

In preparing for a buzz session there are certain responsibilities which must be met by the members of the group. The single most important ingredient for success is knowledge of the subject to be explored. There can be little hope for the discussion group if it becomes no more than a pooling of ignorance. For most occasions there will be a special need or problem which brings the group together. In advance of the meeting, background information should be located to determine the history of the problem and any actions or events which have already taken place that might influence the group in reaching agreements. Participants should examine possible courses of action which might reasonably be decided upon and determine a tentative point of view or course of action which they can support.

Group decision-making is often criticized as being time consuming and slow. This is undoubtedly true, but when people have a hand in making decisions, they are generally more likely to be satisfied and agreeable with the actions taken.

The chairman should carefully prepare a discussion plan in advance of the meeting. He should plan an introduction which establishes the importance of the problem to the members of the group. In the introduction he should further plan on narrowing the scope of the discussion to those areas which he considers to be of prime importance.

During the buzz session the chairman should give all participants opportunity to contribute information and opinions. He must maintain a strict neutrality; he must be fair and honest and recognize and consider minority points of view. Especially at the beginning of the discussion, people are often shy and hesitant. A discussion leader should plan on stimulating interest and ideas at the beginning of and during the discussion by preparing a series of leading questions in advance of the meeting. Another technique for stimulating responses is by directing specific questions to various individuals in the group.

The chairman must be sensitive to the moods and feelings of the group. When the group reaches a decision or agreement, he should accurately state the conclusions reached. If the group reaches a stalemate on a point being discussed, he should close further discussion by stating the areas of disagreement which exist and moving on to another point.

At the end of the discussion the chairman should again restate any conclusions or agreements reached by the group. Any unresolved items or questions should also be noted.

SYMPOSIUM   A more formal type of group discussion is the SYMPOSIUM. In this type of discussion, members of a group co-operatively explore a topic and report their findings to a larger group. The symposium is like *one very large speech given by a number of people.*

In advance of the presentation the members of the group meet and decide upon the broad topic to be discussed. After each member has an opportunity to do general research on the topic, the group will meet for a second time. At the second meeting the topic is again informally discussed and located information is shared. The group then divides the general topic into workable parts or divisions. Each member of the group assumes responsibility for preparing a speech dealing with one of the areas of concern. In preparing each segment for presentation, the members will go through all of the steps discussed in Chapter III. Each speaker will carefully plan and prepare his own speech complete with Introduction, Body, and Conclusion.

The chairman of a symposium has very specific responsibilities. Once the group has decided upon the major areas of the topic to be discussed the chairman also prepares an outline. It is his responsibility to carefully plan an introduction for the total group presentation. In his introduction he must gain the audience's attention and introduce each speaker. As he introduces the speakers, he previews the areas or divisions of the topic to be covered by each. To satisfy the responsibilities of the chairman he must know something about each of the topics and, therefore, he must research *each* of the topics assigned to the members of the group. Following each presentation, the chairman has the job of providing transitions or bridges between the speeches. He should be able to summarize, review, or add information which is pertinent in the transitions. The chairman provides a sense of continuity to the total presentation. In the event that one member of the group is unable to present his portion of the discussion the chairman must be well-enough prepared to fill in the information or material which would otherwise be omitted.

After all of the members of the group have made their speeches, the chairman presents the group's conclusion. At this point, he very briefly reviews the main points made by the group and presents a strong final thought.

FORUM Following a stimulating and interesting group discussion there may be differences of opinion offered or there may be questions which the audience would like answered. This portion of the discussion is called the FORUM. During a forum the audience has an opportunity to state opinions and to ask questions of the "experts." Questions are directed to the chairman. Following the statement of the question, the chairman repeats the question to be sure that it is heard and understood by the members of the group and the audience. The chairman then directs the question to the member of his group who is best qualified to answer.

The intent of the symposium is to provide worthwhile information and knowledge about a topic of significance to an audience. When it is the intent of the group to present differing opinions about a controversial topic another discussion format is used.

ROUND TABLE The ROUND TABLE discussion provides an audience with an opportunity to hear speakers present facts and opinions concerning *opposing sides of* a controversial topic. Though this is a formal kind of group discussion, it is not to be confused with a debate. In a round table discussion an equal number of speakers present arguments and evidence in support of a position they have taken regarding the controversy. Speeches are presented in support of or in opposition to the topic but there is no attempt made during the speeches to answer or refute ideas presented by opposing speakers.

In advance of the presentation, *all* of the speakers meet together to limit, restrict, and narrow the topic. A further purpose of meeting is to check and see that the most important facts and arguments are presented on both sides. Though each speaker attempts to present his most logical and convincing arguments, the *group's* main purpose is *not* to convince or persuade for or against the question being discussed, but to make facts available to the audience so that they can make their own judgement.

In preparation for this type of discussion, once again *all* participants prepare their speeches in the manner previously discussed. Each member of the group prepares his speech outline giving attention to an appropriate Introduction, Body, and Conclusion.

The chairman introduces the topic and relates the subject to the audience's interests. He then previews the controversial nature of the subject and introduces each speaker. The order in which the speeches are given is left up to the group; you may alternate speeches or present all of the speeches for one side followed by the speeches in opposition.

Between each speech the chairman will present his transition information, reviewing the arguments presented and leading the audience's interest to the next speaker. When all of the individual speeches are given, the chairman reviews the major points covered. In his conclusion *he does not attempt to influence the audience's acceptance or rejection of the question being discussed.* His final thought is generally one which indicates that any decision rests with the audience now that they possess facts and information on both sides.

The forum period following the round table discussion is often begun by allowing the members of the group an opportunity to ask questions of each other. As in all questions asked during a forum, they should be carefully thought out and asked as simply and directly as possible. Lengthy preliminary statements should be avoided. *The forum is a question and answer period, not a time for lengthy filibusters.* It is the chairman's responsibility to see that questions asked are pertinent and appropriate. If he feels that someone violates this rule he should interrupt and tactfully suggest that the speaker either get to the question or allow someone else an opportunity to speak.

In all group discussions the chairman's importance cannot be over-emphasized. A good chairman can make an average discussion seem excellent. A poorly prepared chairman can make an otherwise excellent discussion seem like a disaster.

Keep in mind at all times the importance of mutual cooperation and assistance. Group discussion is an effective and efficient device by which people may explore and discover areas of controversy and agreement, reasons for belief or disbelief, and as a basis for valid and sound judgement. Your success as a member of a group is dependent upon the success of all other members of your group. On this note let us turn our attention to another special use of your oral communication.

FUNCTIONING AT MEETINGS

When man first stood erect on his two hind legs and got together with other men in groups, he soon realized that there was need for rules and laws. In that primitive society the first rule which he learned was probably "don't pick a fight with someone bigger or stronger than yourself." The penalty for breaking this first law was likely to be a broken head. As man has become more civilized he has also become more complicated. The same thing has happened to his laws. Today people often find themselves placed in a position where they must work together in large and small groups to accomplish common aims. We soon realize the need for rules and laws if our groups are to function effectively.

In 1876 General Henry M. Robert recognized the need for a manual which would assist groups in establishing rules for functioning in meetings. In the preface to his first edition he wrote, "The object of *Rules of Order* is to assist an assembly to accomplish in the best manner the work for which it was designed . . . Where there is no law, but every man does what is right in his own eyes, there is the least of real liberty."[1]

A study of *Robert's Rules of Order* is a separate course in itself. In this text we shall not attempt a detailed study of parliamentary procedures, but we shall establish some general guide lines to assist you in being a better and more active participant in meetings.

A basic first rule which we shall establish is *that you should use only as many rules as are necessary to accomplish the aims of any group.* Rules are established only to assist you in operating most

1. Robert, Henry M., *Robert's Rules of Order Revised*, Chicago, Scott, Foresman and Company, 1951, p. 14.

effectively. If you can operate with but few rules, by all means, do so. In large groups more elaborate rules are generally required. For you to be an active participant in large groups where strict adherence to parliamentary procedures is followed you must become familiar with some fundamental understandings.

Parliamentary rules are established with three basic concepts in mind: (1) *rules facilitate the efficient handling of business,* (2) *rules provide for the right of the majority to make decisions,* and (3) *the rights of the minority to be heard must not be denied.*

As in most speaking or oral communication situations a logical order of events is desirable. A simplified ORDER OF BUSINESS which covers most situations includes:

1. *Call to order:* At a predetermined time the chairman of the group will call the members to order and announce the business before the group.
2. *Roll call:* In many groups the roll is called to determine the presence or absence of members and to determine the total attendance present.
3. *Reading and approval of minutes:* The secretary's record of the business conducted at the meetings is called the minutes. The minutes of the preceding meeting are read aloud and either approved as read or corrected prior to approval.
4. *Reports of standing committees:* In many organizations it is common practice to have preliminary work done by committees. A committee appointed for a definite period of time and for a definite purpose is a standing committee.
5. *Reports of special committees:* A special committee is appointed for a limited period of time and for only a limited purpose. Once a committee has reported its findings to the group it is generally dismissed.
6. *Unfinished business:* Any business which has been introduced at a previous meeting and then interrupted before final action could be taken on it is called "old business" or unfinished.
7. *New business:* As the name indicates, any business or suggested action which is being brought before the group for the first time is called new business.
8. *Adjournment:* At the completion of all of the business to be acted upon at a meeting, the chairman declares the meeting

adjourned or ended. Any member can at any time make a 'motion to adjourn'; if the motion passes the meeting is ended.

Most groups or organizations which meet on a permanent or regular basis will soon find need for establishing and recording their rules of operation. Those rules which remain unchanged for the group are included in a CONSTITUTION. Those rules which are likely to be changed or modified are included in the BY-LAWS or SPECIAL RULES. Normally included in the constitution would be:

Section I.   The name of the organization and its purposes
Section II.   The qualifications for membership
Section III.   The officers; their duties and election
Section IV.   Determination of meeting dates and times

The by-laws or special rules are generally kept at a minimum. Since there are so many groups to which people belong, it would be most confusing if every group had entirely different rules. It is desirable to have some degree of agreement and uniformity in the operation of various groups. This is generally accomplished by keeping most special rules of operation at a minimum and including in the by-laws a statement which established some well-known guide or manual as the authority in all cases not covered by the special rules of the organization. The manual put out by General Robert in 1876 has been regularly revised and updated many times since it was first printed. *Robert's Rules of Order Revised* is still one of the most commonly used authorities in the field of proper procedures.

Though there are many complicated and confusing rules which can be applied to parliamentary procedures, if you have an understanding of but a few basic rules, you will be able to take an active part in meetings. You should be familiar with the correct procedures for MAKING MOTIONS, AMENDING MOTIONS, and VOTING ON MOTIONS.

MAKING MOTIONS   Motions are classed under four headings: **main motions, subsidiary motions, incidental motions, and privileged motions.** Since our purpose here is to provide you with only a fundamental discussion of parliamentary rules, we shall just define and list the major subsidiary, incidental, and privileged motions, and spend the major part of this discussion talking about main motions.

Main Motions are used to bring any suggestion before a group for discussion and decision. To make a main motion a person must first be recognized and called upon by the chairman. The member then states his proposal, using the phrase, *"I move that . . ."* to introduce his suggestion or recommendation. In order that time not be wasted on discussion of items which are of interest to only one person a "second" is required. Any other person in the group who wants to discuss the motion states, *"I second the motion."* The person who makes a second does not have to wait to be recognized by the chairman. Once a motion has been "moved and seconded" it. is then open for *discussion.* During the discussion of a motion only one person at a time is allowed to speak to the question. The chairman calls upon the person who is to speak and he is said to "have the floor." No one else may discuss the topic until after a speaker has finished his comments. The chairman must be fair and impartial in calling on people who represent both sides of the question. When called upon, a member is allowed to discuss only such information as relates to the topic being discussed.

AMENDING MOTIONS   If a member wished to *change* or *modify* the motion under discussion he may move to "amend the motion." To amend a motion a member of the group must be called upon by the chairman to make his changes. The member states, *"I move to amend the motion by . . ."*. He then may add, change, delete or substitute words or parts of the original motion. An amendment is called a "subsidiary motion." *(Any motion which modifies, changes, delays, or disposes of a main motion is a subsidiary motion.).* The amendment must also be seconded. Once the subsidiary motion is made and seconded it must be discussed and voted upon *before* the original main motion can be disposed of. If the amendment receives a favorable vote, its effect is to change the original motion. If it does not receive a favorable vote the main motion stays as it was before the amendment was offered.

VOTING ON MOTIONS   After the group has had oppor-tunity to discuss the motion or the group votes to stop discussion the chairman has the motion put to a vote. Motions are voted upon in several ways: by **voice, show of hands, standing, ballot, roll call,** or **general consent.** The chairman has the responsibility for taking the vote and announcing the results. If he is not certain of the results he can have the vote retaken, or if he is still in doubt after calling for a voice vote, he may ask for a show of hands or a standing vote. He can not have a vote taken by ballot or roll call unless it is required by the rules of the organization or by a majority decision.

As you can see the amendment is a subsidiary motion. Other such motions include motions "to postpone," "to refer to committee," "to limit discussion," "to vote immediately" and "to put on the table."

Incidental Motions are those which come up as a result of a motion being discussed or acted upon. These motions include "questions of order," "requests for information," and questions about methods of voting. These motions are important to proper handling or deciding on main motions so they can be made during the discussion of the main motion.

Privileged Motions do not relate to the question or motion being discussed but these motions are considered so important that *they can interrupt other discussion* and other business being carried on. These motions include "questions of rights or privileges," "the motion to adjourn" and "the motion to recess."

With these basics of parliamentary procedures you should be able to be an active participant in meetings. Your oral communication's knowledges and skills will all be called upon in meetings. To do a good job in effectively presenting future proposals you will call upon your knowledge of **the informative speech.** To explain your stand during discussion you will use your **persuasive skills.** You will use your skill in **reading aloud** when making committee reports. You will use your knowledge of **group discussion** when serving on committees. Finally, you will use all of your skill and ability as an effective speaker when you are appointed or elected to the position of chairman or presiding officer of the groups to which you belong.

SUMMARY

A full, rich, and rewarding existence in our society demands an interchange of thoughts, ideas, and opinions. In this chapter we have explored three of the most common forms of social interaction: ORAL REPORTS, GROUP DECISION-MAKING, and the FORMAL MEETING.

Skill in these more specialized uses of oral communications is an outgrowth of the fundamental skills which have been examined in the preceding five chapters.

For you to achieve maximum and consistent success as an effective oral communicator you must give careful attention to the three basics of every speech presentation: CONTENT, ORGANI-ZATION, and DELIVERY. First, you must have something of importance to communicate to your listener. Second, you must have a logical and orderly arrangement of your ideas. And, you must possess the necessary skill to present your ideas effectively. All are important; none must be overlooked.

Habits are acquired over a long period of time. You must continue to work for mastery of good speech habits in every situation. Continue to be aware of your poor speech habits and work toward replacing them with the better habits of which you are now aware. The rewards of meaningful and effective communication will be yours and they will serve you throughout your entire life.

ACTIVITIES AND SKILL DRILLS:

1. Group discussions may be formal (as discussed in this chapter) or informal. Meet together in small groups of three to five people and informally discuss a topic for formal presentation to your class. Select a topic which is of interest to your group and to your audience. Decide upon the best format to use (symposium or round table). Decide on each person's responsibilities in the discussion presentation. To avoid duplication, select one person to report back to the class the decisions which you make.

2. Using the decisions made in activity #1, research and prepare for a formal group discussion. Each member of the group, including the chairman, should prepare an outline and do research on his agreed-upon area of concern. Allow time for a forum period following your group presentation.

3. Using the suggestions in this chapter as a guide, organize the class into a speech club. Establish a constitution and by-laws. Conduct regular business meetings; practice making, seconding and discussing motions. Change the chairman after each motion to allow each person an opportunity to function as chairman.

APPENDIX

A

ADVANCED ASSIGNMENTS*

*Note: The inclusion of a 'Grade Value' at the beginning of each of the following assignments is an attempt to establish a relative value for these communication experiences. The technique or method used for assigning weight to this factor is left to the discretion of the individual instructor.

SPEECH NO. 1 : Introduction

TIME LIMITS : 2 to 3 minutes

GRADE VALUE : 5 points

GENERAL PURPOSE:

The aim of this speech is to enable you to become better acquainted with the members of the class in general and one member of your class in particular.

SPECIFIC ASSIGNMENT:

1. Locate a member of the class with whom you are not now acquainted.

2. Conduct cross-interviews. You will interview your partner; he will interview you.

3. Discover the important, the interesting, and the unusual about your partner. What makes him or her a unique and individual personality?

4. Prepare an outline after you have gathered your facts. Plan the order in which your interesting material is to be presented. Decide how you will begin and end your presentation. Outlines will be turned into the instructor before you begin your speech presentation.

5. Prepare a 3 x 5 card with your delivery notes. You will be permitted to use only one side of one 3 x 5 card for this assignment.

6. Rehearse your presentation aloud to insure that you will be able to say what you want to say effectively and to establish that you will be able to stay within the time limits of the assignment.

EVALUATION:

1. Each speaker will be graded and evaluated primarily upon delivery in this assignment.

2. Outlines will be checked and returned but will not be graded.

SPEECH NO. 2   :   The Controversial Topic

TIME LIMITS   :   4 to 6 minutes

GRADE VALUE   :   15 points

GENERAL PURPOSE:

The aim of this speech is to lead you to explore a topic about which your audience may have contradictory points of view. You will be expected to carefully study the subject and take a stand relative to your subject.

SPECIFIC ASSIGNMENT:

1. Select a topic around which there exists differences of opinion or differing points of view.

2. After a careful analysis of the total subject, determine your position in relation to the topic and be prepared to present and support your point of view.

3. Research your topic fully and be prepared to defend, support, and *convince* your audience to accept your position relative to the topic.

4. Locate and utilize effectively at least five different forms of verbal supporting material to lend authority and verification to your position. In the left hand margin of your outline identify each of the various forms of support.

5. At the end of your outline list in proper bibliographical form the sources you have used in preparation of your speech. You are required to cite, as a minimum, two published sources.

EVALUATION:

1. One-third of your grade will be determined by your effective utilization of delivery techniques.

2. One-third of your grade will be an evaluation of correct outline organization. Carefully check the use of correct headings, notations, identification of support forms, adequacy of detail, depth of coverage, and use of bibliography.

3. One-third of your grade on this assignment will be determined by your audience's ability to recognize and correctly identify the five different forms of verbal support which you utilize in your presentation.

*SPECIAL NOTE: Beginning with this speech and on all subsequent speech outlines you will be required to include; (1) an identification of *support forms* in the left margin, and (2) a bibliography at the end of your paper with a minimum of two published sources.

SPEECH NO. 3   :   Speech to Inform

TIME LIMITS   :   3 to 5 minutes

GRADE VALUE   :   15 points

GENERAL PURPOSE:

The aim of this speech is to increase your audience's information and knowledge on a topic of interest and significance.

SPECIFIC ASSIGNMENT:

1. Carefully analyze your own interests and the interests of your audience. Plan to present some new information and new ideas to your audience.

2. You will be expected to use visual aids in this presentation to aid audience understanding. Your aids must not dominate the presentation; rather it should clarify, elaborate, or develop the points which you plan to discuss.

3. Prepare an outline and note cards to assist you in determining the proper order of points and to insure adequate coverage of your subject. There is no limit to the number of cards you may use on this assignment. Do not use the back of your cards.

4. Practice your presentation aloud to insure effective discussion of material, proper utilization of your aids, and proper timing.

EVALUATION:

1. One-third of your grade will be based upon delivery, with particular emphasis being given to the delivery techniques discussed following your last presentation.

2. Your effective utilization of correct outline technique and procedure will be evaluated.

3. An evaluation will be made of the content of your presentation, the discussion of your information and the proper utilization of your visual aids.

SPEECH NO. 4   :   Oral Interpretation

TIME LIMITS   :   5 to 7 minutes

GRADE VALUE   :   15 points

GENERAL PURPOSE:

The aim of this speech is to entertain your audience through the interpretation of literature utilizing the lecture-recital format.

SPECIFIC ASSIGNMENT:

1. Locate, study carefully, and select material from two or more authors which, presented with your extemporaneous introduction, transitions, and conclusion, develop a unified central theme. Your selections may of necessity be required to be cut in order to satisfy the time requirements.

2. As a result of your reading and interpreting the literature and through your presentation of original comments, plan to provide your audience with the full intent and significance of the literature presented.

3. As a result of your careful study and analysis of your prose or poetry, and with due consideration of your original material, you should plan to create for your audience an emotional satisfaction and an intellectual appreciation for the important and significant content values of the material.

EVALUATION:

1. One-third of your grade will be determined by the choice and arrangement of the materials (**organization**). Attention will be given to your choice of material in that is should provide your audience with greater insight into the literature than the audience would gain from a casual reading of the same materials.

2. One-third of your grade will be determined primarily by the speaker's skill in communicating the extemporaneous portions of

the presentation (delivery). The dynamic elements of pitch, volume, pause, vocal quality, posture, and expression throughout the entire presentation will be evaluated.

3. One-third of the grade will be determined by the speaker's ability to establish and project the *author's* ideas and attitudes (content). Attention should be given to understanding the author's imagery, references, and allusions, and to appropriate phrasing, emphasis, and articulation to communicate the appropriate moods, attitudes, and emotions.

SPEECH NO. 5 : Group Discussion

TIME LIMITS : 5 to 6 minutes per individual

GRADE VALUE : 15 points

GENERAL PURPOSE:

The aim of this speech is to present a more thorough and complete coverage of a topic of significance than ordinarily would be possible by a single speaker.

SPECIFIC ASSIGNMENT:

1. The class will be divided into groups of 3 to 5 students for this activity.

2. Two class periods will be provided for you to work cooperatively with your group.
   a. 1st meeting.
      (1) Select a chairman from your group.
      (2) One member of the group should function as a recorder for the group to make notes of any decisions made by the group.
      (3) Agree upon a topic of significance to be presented.
      (4) Tentatively agree upon the type of group discussion which you plan to present.
      (5) Each member of the group will be responsible for doing general research on the topic chosen. Bring your bibliography and selected materials to the next scheduled meeting of your group.
   b. 2nd meeting.
      (1) Discuss your topic informally; share the results of your research and determine those areas which require additional research.
      (2) Assign individual responsibilities to the members of your group. Be certain that each person understands the extent and limits of his responsibility.
      (3) Make a final determination of the type of group discussion you plan to present and the areas of the topic which you will cover.

(4) At the end of this second meeting plan to turn in to the instructor the following information:
(a) Topic to be discussed.
(b) Chairman's name.
(c) Names of each member of the group and their individual areas of responsibility.
(d) Type of group discussion to be presented.

3. Each member of the group will be expected to prepare an outline which covers his area of responsibility. The same format and technique as employed in previous speeches will be employed.

EVALUATION:

1. Each member of the group will be evaluated upon his individual presentation. Particular attention will be given to the extent and degree of individual participation, delivery skill, and content.

2. Each member of the group, including the chairman, is required to turn in an outline which will be graded. The chairman's outline will be expected to show his individual and separate research on the topic to be discussed.

3. A group grade will be given on the total effectiveness of your presentation as evidenced by the balance of content, relationship of presentations, and individual contributations toward the overall effectiveness of the presentation.

SPEECH NO. 6	:	Persuasive Speech
TIME LIMITS	:	5 to 7 minutes
GRADE VALUE	:	15 points

GENERAL PURPOSE:

The aim of this presentation is to change your audience's point of view or beliefs about a topic of significance. In this speech you will combine emotional appeals with intellectual appeals to achieve your purpose.

SPECIFIC ASSIGNMENT:

1. Carefully analyze your audience prior to selecting your topic to determine its existing attitudes and beliefs.

2. Plan to relate your topic to your audience in order to establish a feeling of empathy or personal involvement.

3. In locating materials for this presentation, in addition to content which appeals to the intellect, seek out those topics and materials which possess strong emotional stimuli; such as, fear, anger, love.

4. Your ultimate objective in this presentation is to influence human behavior; to move your audience to think, to experience, to believe, to enjoy, to act—in short, to respond as you wish them to respond.

EVALUATION:

1. Effective utilization of the mechanical aspects of delivery.

2. Proper organizational technique as evidenced on proper outline structure.

3. Degree of audience involvement and speaker's ability to change or modify audience's beliefs or attitudes through effective use of content and material.

SPEECH NO. 7   :   Impromptu

TIME LIMITS   :

GRADE VALUE   :   10 points

GENERAL PURPOSE:

The aim of this speech is to develop skill in organizing your thoughts in an "on the spur of the moment situation."

SPECIFIC ASSIGNMENT:

1. Organization time for this speech will be determined by and limited to the length of time that the speaker who precedes you takes with his presentation.

2. Speech topics will be distributed for presentation.

3. Organization, as time permits, would include:
   a. A determination of a specific purpose which you plan to achieve.
   b. An effective opening statement.
   c. Major divisions of the topic to be discussed.
   d. A summary close.

4. You will be allowed to use one side of one 3 x 5 card to record any notes which you consider to be necessary.

EVALUATION:

1. You will be evaluated upon your poise and control as demonstrated by delivery technique.

2. Your ability to quickly organize and effectively present a logical and organized presentation will be evaluated.

SPEECH NO. 8 : Final Speech

TIME LIMITS : 8 to 10 minutes

GRADE VALUE : 25 points

GENERAL PURPOSE:

The purpose of this speech is to provide you with an opportunity to demonstrate the skill and ability which you have acquired and now possess as an effective speaker. Attention should be given to all of the methods and techniques presented and discussed during this semester.

SPECIFIC ASSIGNMENT:

1. You are free to choose any topic to achieve any purpose for your final presentation.

2. Carefully select your purpose for this final assignment. You will be required to turn in to the instructor, approximately two weeks prior to the beginning of this assignment, a statement of your purpose. The general area of concern, as well as the specific divisions of your topic, should be determined.

3. This presentation is the culmination of all that you have been expected to learn. Use this opportunity to demonstrate the highest level of skill and technique which you now possess.

EVALUATION:

1. Outlines are required as evidence of your organizational skill, depth of research, and use of supporting data, but your outline will not be corrected or graded.

2. Grades will be determined by the use of the objective rating chart (see Appendix B) which will evaluate specific areas of accomplishment.

3. This final evaluation will be based upon your skill as evaluated against college speakers in general who have completed a fundamentals course in speech.

APPENDIX
B
EVALUATION FORMS

ORAL COMMUNICATIONS CRITIQUE

The following set of evaluation forms has been prepared to provide the student and the instructor with a means of evaluating the growth and progress of the individual student towards more effective oral communication. In preparing for each assignment the student should complete the upper portion of one form with his name, speech purpose, assignment number, and the date. When called upon to speak, the student will give the evaluation form and his outline to the instructor. During the speech presentation the instructor will indicate, for each student, the degree and extent of success experienced by the speaker in meeting the special areas of concern for the assignment by placing a check in each appropriate box on the form. Space is provided for the instructor to make more specific comments and suggestions for consideration by the student. Through a comparison of succeeding evaluation forms, the student should be able to see a pattern of strengths and weaknesses. To assist the student in more easily and vividly observing his growth a semester evaluation graph is included. When the individual evaluation forms are returned to the student, he should place a mark in each appropriate box for the particular assignment on the semester evaluation graph. At the end of the course the semester evaluation graph will be turned in to the instructor as an aid in making a final evaluation of the student's growth and progress.

SEMESTER EVALUATION

NAME: _____

Speech Number	1	2	3	4	5	6	7	8	9	10

ORGANIZATION

23–25										
18–22										
13–17										
8–12										
0–7										

DELIVERY

23–25										
18–22										
13–17										
8–12										
0–7										

CONTENT

23–25										
18–22										
13–17										
8–12										
0–7										

ORAL COMMUNICATIONS CRITIQUE

NAME:_____

SPEECH PURPOSE:_____

ASSIGNMENT NUMBER:_____ DATE:_____

Ratings: 5–Superior, 4–Excellent, 3–Good, 2–Fair, 1–Poor

ORGANIZATION	5	4	3	2	1	COMMENTS
Attention step						
Preview						
Discussion						
Review						
Final thought						

ORGANIZATION TOTAL_____

DELIVERY	5	4	3	2	1	
Posture						
Audience contact						
Vocal variety						
Articulation						
Movement and Gestures						

DELIVERY TOTAL_____

CONTENT	5	4	3	2	1	
Clarity of purpose						
Adequacy of support						
Arrangement of ideas						
Effective transitions						
Adaptation to audience						

CONTENT TOTAL_____

23–25 superior
18–22 above average
13–17 average
 8–12 below average
 0–7 inferior

ORAL COMMUNICATIONS CRITIQUE

NAME:_____

SPEECH PURPOSE:_____

ASSIGNMENT NUMBER:_____ DATE:_____

Ratings: 5–Superior, 4–Excellent, 3–Good, 2–Fair, 1–Poor

ORGANIZATION   5   4   3   2   1   COMMENTS

Attention step

Preview

Discussion

Review

Final thought

ORGANIZATION TOTAL_____

DELIVERY   5   4   3   2   1

Posture

Audience contact

Vocal variety

Articulation

Movement and Gestures

DELIVERY TOTAL_____

CONTENT   5   4   3   2   1

Clarity of purpose

Adequacy of support

Arrangement of ideas

Effective transitions

Adaptation to audience

CONTENT TOTAL_____

23–25 superior
18–22 above average
13–17 average
 8–12 below average
 0–7 inferior

ORAL COMMUNICATIONS CRITIQUE

NAME:_____

SPEECH PURPOSE:_____

ASSIGNMENT NUMBER:_____ DATE:_____

Ratings: 5-Superior, 4-Excellent, 3-Good, 2-Fair, 1-Poor

ORGANIZATION   5   4   3   2   1   COMMENTS

Attention step

Preview

Discussion

Review

Final thought

ORGANIZATION
TOTAL_____

DELIVERY   5   4   3   2   1

Posture

Audience contact

Vocal variety

Articulation

Movement and Gestures

DELIVERY
TOTAL_____

CONTENT   5   4   3   2   1

Clarity of purpose

Adequacy of support

Arrangement of ideas

Effective transitions

Adaptation to audience

CONTENT
TOTAL_____

23-25 superior
18-22 above average
13-17 average
8-12 below average
0-7   inferior

ORAL COMMUNICATIONS CRITIQUE

NAME:_____

SPEECH PURPOSE:_____

ASSIGNMENT NUMBER:_____ DATE:_____

Ratings: 5–Superior, 4–Excellent, 3–Good, 2–Fair, 1–Poor

ORGANIZATION	5	4	3	2	1	COMMENTS
Attention step						
Preview						
Discussion						
Review						
Final thought						

ORGANIZATION TOTAL_____

DELIVERY	5	4	3	2	1
Posture					
Audience contact					
Vocal variety					
Articulation					
Movement and Gestures					

DELIVERY TOTAL_____

CONTENT	5	4	3	2	1
Clarity of purpose					
Adequacy of support					
Arrangement of ideas					
Effective transitions					
Adaptation to audience					

CONTENT TOTAL_____

23–25 superior
18–22 above average
13–17 average
8–12 below average
0–7 inferior

ORAL COMMUNICATIONS CRITIQUE

NAME:_____

SPEECH PURPOSE:_____

ASSIGNMENT NUMBER:_____ DATE:_____

Ratings: 5–Superior, 4–Excellent, 3–Good, 2–Fair, 1–Poor

ORGANIZATION	5	4	3	2	1	COMMENTS
Attention step						
Preview						
Discussion						
Review						
Final thought						ORGANIZATION TOTAL_____

DELIVERY	5	4	3	2	1	
Posture						
Audience contact						
Vocal variety						
Articulation						
Movement and Gestures						DELIVERY TOTAL_____

CONTENT	5	4	3	2	1	
Clarity of purpose						
Adequacy of support						
Arrangement of ideas						
Effective transitions						
Adaptation to audience						CONTENT TOTAL_____

23–25 superior
18–22 above average
13–17 average
 8–12 below average
 0–7   inferior

ORAL COMMUNICATIONS CRITIQUE

NAME:_____

SPEECH PURPOSE:_____

ASSIGNMENT NUMBER:_____ DATE:_____

Ratings: 5–Superior, 4–Excellent, 3–Good, 2–Fair, 1–Poor

ORGANIZATION   5   4   3   2   1   COMMENTS

Attention step

Preview

Discussion

Review

Final thought

ORGANIZATION TOTAL_____

DELIVERY   5   4   3   2   1

Posture

Audience contact

Vocal variety

Articulation

Movement and Gestures

DELIVERY TOTAL_____

CONTENT   5   4   3   2   1

Clarity of purpose

Adequacy of support

Arrangement of ideas

Effective transitions

Adaptation to audience

CONTENT TOTAL_____

23–25 superior
18–22 above average
13–17 average
8–12 below average
0–7 inferior

ORAL COMMUNICATIONS CRITIQUE

NAME:_____

SPEECH PURPOSE:_____

ASSIGNMENT NUMBER:_____ DATE:_____

Ratings: 5-Superior, 4-Excellent, 3-Good, 2-Fair, 1-Poor

ORGANIZATION	5	4	3	2	1	COMMENTS
Attention step						
Preview						
Discussion						
Review						
Final thought						

ORGANIZATION TOTAL _____

DELIVERY	5	4	3	2	1
Posture					
Audience contact					
Vocal variety					
Articulation					
Movement and Gestures					

DELIVERY TOTAL_____

CONTENT	5	4	3	2	1
Clarity of purpose					
Adequacy of support					
Arrangement of ideas					
Effective transitions					
Adaptation to audience					

CONTENT TOTAL_____

23-25 superior
18-22 above average
13-17 average
8-12 below average
0-7 inferior

ORAL COMMUNICATIONS CRITIQUE

NAME:_____

SPEECH PURPOSE:_____

ASSIGNMENT NUMBER:_____ DATE:_____

Ratings: 5–Superior, 4–Excellent, 3–Good, 2–Fair, 1–Poor

ORGANIZATION	5	4	3	2	1	COMMENTS
Attention step						
Preview						
Discussion						
Review						
Final thought						

ORGANIZATION TOTAL _____

DELIVERY	5	4	3	2	1	
Posture						
Audience contact						
Vocal variety						
Articulation						
Movement and Gestures						

DELIVERY TOTAL_____

CONTENT	5	4	3	2	1	
Clarity of purpose						
Adequacy of support						
Arrangement of ideas						
Effective transitions						
Adaptation to audience						

CONTENT TOTAL_____

23–25 superior
18–22 above average
13–17 average
8–12 below average
0–7 inferior

ORAL COMMUNICATIONS CRITIQUE

NAME:_____

SPEECH PURPOSE:_____

ASSIGNMENT NUMBER:_____ DATE:_____

Ratings: 5–Superior, 4–Excellent, 3–Good, 2–Fair, 1–Poor

ORGANIZATION	5	4	3	2	1	COMMENTS
Attention step						
Preview						
Discussion						
Review						
Final thought						

ORGANIZATION TOTAL_____

DELIVERY	5	4	3	2	1
Posture					
Audience contact					
Vocal variety					
Articulation					
Movement and Gestures					

DELIVERY TOTAL_____

CONTENT	5	4	3	2	1
Clarity of purpose					
Adequacy of support					
Arrangement of ideas					
Effective transitions					
Adaptation to audience					

CONTENT TOTAL_____

23–25 superior
18–22 above average
13–17 average
 8–12 below average
 0–7   inferior

ORAL COMMUNICATIONS CRITIQUE

NAME:_____

SPEECH PURPOSE:_____

ASSIGNMENT NUMBER:_____ DATE:_____

Ratings: 5–Superior, 4–Excellent, 3–Good, 2–Fair, 1–Poor

ORGANIZATION	5	4	3	2	1	COMMENTS
Attention step						
Preview						
Discussion						
Review						
Final thought						

ORGANIZATION TOTAL_____

DELIVERY	5	4	3	2	1
Posture					
Audience contact					
Vocal variety					
Articulation					
Movement and Gestures					

DELIVERY TOTAL_____

CONTENT	5	4	3	2	1
Clarity of purpose					
Adequacy of support					
Arrangement of ideas					
Effective transitions					
Adaptation to audience					

CONTENT TOTAL_____

23–25 superior
18–22 above average
13–17 average
8–12 below average
0–7 inferior

APPENDIX 'C'
STUDENT OUTLINES AND SPEECHES*

*Note: The un-edited outlines and speeches included in this section were prepared by students enrolled in a basic oral communications class at San Diego City College during fall semester, 1967. They are offered for your critical examination and evaluation. The speech on "Unwed Mothers" was prepared by Helen Harvey, "Public Apathy" was prepared by Leon Tipton.

SPEECH OUTLINE

Purpose: To inform the audience of the problems facing unwed mothers; public criticism, discrimination, indifference.

INTRODUCTION

I. A pregnant girl's flight

   A. Average appearance

   1. Young (mid-20's)

   2. Well-dressed

   3. Soft spoken

   4. Educated accent

   B. Seeking refuge

   1. Maternity shelter

   2. Escaping ostracism

   C. Typical of unwed mothers

   1. Flee home

      a. No protection

      b. No money

   2. Several thousand every year

II. Problems facing unwed mothers

   A. Public criticism

   B. Discrimination

   C. Indifference

BODY

I. Public criticism

  A. Born bad

    1. Explanation for unwed mother

    2. Sinful behavior to be expected

  B. Threat to society

    1. Willfully bypassed convention

    2. Threatens security of legal family

  C. Branded as oversexed

  D. Presumed mentally dull

II. Discrimination

  A. Isolation

    1. Mother promiscuous

      a. Shut off

      b. Stigmatized

    2. "Child of sin"

      a. Child labeled bastard

      b. Morally inferior

  B. No financial help

    1. Aid means condoning sin

    2. Man responsible

      a. Mother usually must name father

      b. Denial results in public trial

    3. Endless red tape

      a. Referrals from one agency to another

      b. Obsolete residence laws

III. Indifference

    A. "By and large we have never taken kindly to paying for the weaknesses and crippling problems of those for whom we were not immediately and legally responsible."

    B. Laws outmoded

        1. "... the laws reflect the attitudes of the past more faithfully than the needs of the present."

        2. Change in laws not likely.

    C. Agencies unconcerned

        1. Adoption stressed

            a. Farm out baby quickly

            b. Avoid undue contact

        2. Little psychological help

            a. Case closed after adoption

            b. Mother "cured" with adoption

CONCLUSION

I. Problems of unwed mothers

    A. Public criticism

    B. Discrimination

    C. Indifference

II. Reforms vitally necessary

    A. Change in laws

    B. Greater public understanding

Bibliography

Young, Leontine. Out of Wedlock. New York: McGraw-Hill Book Company, Inc., 1954.

SPEECH MANUSCRIPT

The girl was young, in her mid-twenties, quiety attractive, and well dressed. Her voice was soft with an educated accent. Only the lines of strain marking her face distinguished her from the average girl. She was an unwed mother to be, seeking a haven in a maternity shelter. She had fled from her hometown to escape the whispers and curious stares of the community.

She is typical of the several thousand unmarried mothers who every year run away from home. They came to the large cities without protection, often without money.

Today I would like to discuss the tremendous problems confronting unwed mothers. I will touch upon three of the basic problems; public criticism, the discrimination against unmarried mothers and their children, and lastly the indifference of society.

Our society today has not progressed one bit in their understanding of the unwed mother. Just as in the time of Hawthorne's Scarlett Letter we denounce the unwed mother as being born bad. So her sinful behavior is to be expected. We consider these girls as a threat to society. We decry their willfully bypassing convention. We tremble in fear at the thought of our precious legal families being torn asunder by this menace. We accuse these girls of being shamelessly over-sexed. We even go so far as to claim they are mentally dull. And yet for all our cries we do nothing to help ease the situation.

Rather we discriminate against them. The mother we brand promiscuous. We completely shut her off from society. She is a tainted woman in our eyes. And the child, this "child of sin" we label a bastard. We mark him for the rest of his life as being morally inferior.

There is little if any financial help for the unwed mother. Giving them aid would mean condoning their sin. So we charge the man with complete responsibility. In many cases, girls attempting to get even the minimum of general welfare are forced to name the father of their child before Uncle Sam will condescend to give them the paltry sum. Denial by the man results in a humiliating public trial. We have devised an endless forest of red tape for our own enjoyment. Referrals from one agency to another and obsolete residence laws are but two examples.

Our indifference is pointed out in Leontine Young's statement: "By and large we have never taken kindly to paying for the weaknesses and crippling problems of those for whom we were not immediately and legally responsible." In other words, why foist their problems on us?! Our sentiments are reflected in the outmoded laws concerning unwed mothers which abound throughout the United States. Young has said that our ". . . laws reflect the attitudes of the past more faithfully than the needs of the present."

The various agencies are unconcerned with either the mother or the child. They stress adoption. Farm out the kid quickly; avoid undue contact with this diseased couple. The case is closed immediately following adoption of the baby. No psychological help is offered. It is assumed that the mother is "cured" as soon as the incriminating evidence is gotten rid of.

Today I have discussed the problems facing unwed mothers and their children. I have tried to show you something of the criticism, discrimination, and indifference dished out by our society. I for one am completely disgusted with myself and the rest of society for our total lack of feeling. I feel reforms are vitally necessary. We definitely need a change in the laws governing unwed mothers. But far more importantly, we need greater public understanding. I intend to seek for reforms. Won't you also?

SPEECH OUTLINE

PURPOSE: To convince the audience of the social decline in the United States caused by public apathy; by discussing the causes, some of the effects, and some possible solutions for public apathy.

INTRODUCTION

I. Headlines

  A. "Bystanders turn faces while girl is hacked to death"

  B. "People on subway read papers while old man is beaten to death"

II. Public Apathy

  A. Causes

  B. Some effects

  C. Possible solutions

BODY

I. Causes

  A. Rising tide of mediocrity

    1. Charles H. Brower

      a. Area of great goof-off

      b. Age of half done job

    2. Mediocrity in education

      a. Instructors force personal ideals on students

        (1) In name of higher knowledge

        (2) Attack on methods or actions

        (3) Attack on academic freedom

      b. Students sell out to instructors

      c. Anything for a grade

         (1) Wearing mini-skirts

         (2) Buying answers to final exams

  3. Mediocrity in politics

      a. Allow "No Choice" candidates

      b. Stay away from polls

B. Personal non-involvement

  1. Admiral Arleigh Burke

      a. Nation and people

      b. Not involved in anything

      c. Lost willingness to compete

      d. Not very strong convictions

  2. National attitude

      a. Selfish

      b. What's in it for me

  3. Miami, Florida

      a. Police officer

         (1) Dresses in street clothes

         (2) Handcuffed

      b. Rode city bus

         (1) From police station

         (2) Rode four blocks

      c. Passengers interviewed

         (1) Saw handcuffs

         (2) None of their business

      d. Whose business

II. Some effects

    A. In San Diego

        1. 600% increase in juvenile narcotics arrests

            a. Parents not aware

            b. Too busy with self goals

            c. Some don't care

        2. 6 million dollar yearly budget

        3. Councilmen paid 5 thousand dollars a year

            a. Halftime effort

            b. Halftime wage

    B. In California

        1. Governor must have bullet proof glass

            a. In office

            b. For protection

        2. State legislature

            a. Can't hold session

            b. Without armed band

            c. Invading chambers

        3. Los Angeles bus companies

            a. Threaten to stop services

                (1) Some areas of city

            b. Unless armed guards on buses

            c. To prevent robberies

    C. In National Capitol

        1. Washington D.C.

            a. Can't walk city streets

        (1) After dark

        (2) Except in well-lighted areas

    b. Fear of being molested

  2. Police become victims of apathy

    a. Two San Fransisco Police Officers

    b. Burglar caught in act

    c. One officer wounded

    d. Suspect arrested

        (1) Tried

        (2) Convicted

        (3) Sent to prison

    e. Officers investigated three times

        (1) Once by Police Department

        (2) Twice by FBI

        (3) Brutality claim

        (4) Cleared of all charges

    f. Not strange if officers look other way

III. Possible solutions

  A. Must re-think responsibilities

    1. Elect and support good governmental officials

      a. Aware of legislative action

      b. Let legislators know feelings on laws

      c. Communicate

    2. Provide better law enforcement

      a. Attract better personnel

b. Education

(1) Police officers

(2) Citizens

B. Must re-think Morality

1. Albert Nevins

a. Morality is determined by self interest

b. Get away from What's in it for me attitude

(1) Get involved in society

(2) Rational and responsible manner

CONCLUSION

I. Apathy

A. Causes

B. Some effects

C. Possible solutions

II. Must stop social decline

A. To continue as a nation

B. Kill public apathy

C. Albert Nevins

1. Individual apathy

Bibliography

Dudley, Guilford Jr., "Self-Reliance or Self-Destruction",

Vital Speeches, August 1, 1965, 31:532-631.

NEVINS, Albert II, "Responsiblity to Mankind",

Vital Speeches, December 1, 1962, 29:117-120.

Shawcross, Lord, New York Times Magazine, June 13, 1965, 44.

SPEECH MANUSCRIPT

Not long ago these headlines glared out at us from the newspaper, "BYSTANDERS TURN THEIR HEADS WHILE YOUNG GIRL WAS HACKED TO DEATH BY RAPIST" and "PASSENGERS ON SUBWAY READ NEWSPAPERS WHILE OLD MAN IS BEATEN TO DEATH BY TEEN HOODLUMS." These tragic incidents did not happen in some foreign country, they happened right here in our United States. The cause of these incidents is PUBLIC APATHY. An anonymous author once wrote, "The history of all democratic societies has been from bondage to spiritual faith, from spiritual faith to courage, from courage to freedom, from freedom to abundance, from abundance to selfishness, from selfishness to apathy, from apathy to dependency, from dependency to bondage". We have reached the stage of SELFISHNESS and APATHY.

This morning I am going to discuss three different aspects of PUBLIC APATHY, Those being the Causes, some of the Effects, and some Possible Solutions to PUBLIC APATHY.

There are two major causes of public apathy, MEDIOCRITY and PERSONAL NONINVOLVEMENT. Charles H. Brower, the president of a nationally known advertising firm has stated, "Here in America we have reached the high tide of mediocrity; the area of the great goof-off; the age of the half done job. The land from coast to coast has been enjoying a stampede away from responsibility. It is populated by the laundry man who won't iron shirts'; with executives whose minds are on the golf course; with teachers who demand a single salary schedule so that achievement cannot be rewarded, nor poor work punished; with students who take cinch courses because the hard ones make them think; with spiritual delinquents of all kinds who have been triumphantly determined to enjoy what has become known as the New Leisure".

Mediocrity has crept into our educational system by teachers and professors forcing their personal ideals onto students instead of teaching. They do this in the name of higher knowledge and any attack on their methods or actions is considered an attack on their academic freedom. The student is adding to this mediocrity by selling out to the instructor. In many cases, the student will do anything, from wearing a mini-skirt and sitting in the front row to buying answers to final examinations, to get a grade.

We are allowing mediocrity to invade politics by allowing the political parties to put NO CHOICE candidates on the ballot, and then we stay away from the polls using these no choice candidates as our excuse.

Admiral Arleigh Burke once said, "As a nation and a people, we don't seem to want to become involved in anything. We seem to have lost the willingness to compete. We want to be liked, we want to be loved, but we don't want to stand up for our convictions. In fact, we don't even want to have very strong convictions". We seem to have taken on the selfish attitude of WHAT'S IN IT FOR ME. A perfect example of this non-involvement happened just this last week in Miami, Florida. A police officer dressed in street clothes and with his hands handcuffed, left the Police Station and boarded a city bus that had stopped in front of the City Jail. He made no effort to hide the handcuffs while he rode the bus for about four blocks. After he left the bus, some of the passengers were interviewed. Most of them stated they saw the man wearing handcuffs, but didn't think it was any of their business. JUST WHOSE BUSINESS IS IT?

Now that we understand how MEDIOCRITY and PERSONAL NON-INVOLVEMENT cause PUBLIC APATHY, just what are some of the effects of public apathy?

Here in San Diego in the last year alone there was a 600 per cent increase in the arrest of juvenile narcotics offenders. I believe that this situation is caused by parents who are so busy accomplishing their own goals, that they don't have time to be aware of the actions of their children. In some cases, the parents don't even want to know what their children are doing and seem to go by the old saying "Ignorance is Bliss".

We live in a city with an annual budget of over 6 million dollars and yet we are only willing to pay the executives who manage this budget the meager sum of 5 thousands a year to do this job. We can only expect a part time effort from these people when we are only willing to pay a part time wage.

I suggest that our society is in a sad state when here in California the governor must have bullet proof glass in his office windows for protection; or when the state legislature cannot meet without having an armed militant gang invade their chambers; or when bus companies in Los Angeles must threaten to discontinue service to some parts of the city unless armed guards are placed on the buses to prevent robberies.

It is also a sad state of affairs when a person in our nation's capital can't take a walk on the city streets, after dark, except in the most well lighted areas without the fear of being robbed or molested.

Even our police officers are becoming victims of this widespread apathy. Take the case of the two San Fransicso police officers who surprised a man in the act of committing a burglary. While the officers were attempting to arrest the suspect, one of the officers had his gun taken away and was wounded by the suspect. The suspect was finally apprehended by the officers, without injury to him. The suspect was then tried, convicted, and sent to prison, but because a claim of Police Brutality had been lodged during the trial, the Police Department investigated the incident and completely cleared the two officers of the brutality charge. The situation did not end at this point. Through the instigation of the American Civil Liberties Union the brutality claim was again brought and another investigation of the incident was made, this time by the FBI. When they completed their investigation, they also found that no brutality had occurred during the arrest. The American Civil Liberties Union then brought the charge that the two police officers had violated the burglar's civil rights while making the arrest. This charge again subjected the two police officers to another investigation by the FBI, and again they were completely cleared. Just think of the pressures placed on not only the police officers, but on their families as well while these investigations were being made. Under these circumstances, it is not strange at all to find that some police officers would rather look the other way and not become involved in an incident for fear that they themselves would in effect be put on trial for doing their jobs.

Now that we have seen how public apathy affects us, how do we solve this problem of public apathy and stop the decline of our society?

I would suggest that we must first re-think our responsibilities. We must be willing to elect and support good governmental officials. We must make ourselves aware of what is going on in both our local and national legislatures and we must let our legislators know how we feel toward the type of laws they are passing. In other words, we must learn to communicate with each other.

We must also provide better law enforcement for ourselves by making this job more attractive to a higher grade of personnel and through education. Education not only of the police officer, but also of ourselves as citizens.

We must then re-think our morality. Albert Nevins has stated, "Morality is determined by self-interest". We must become personally involved in the workings of our society and free ourselves of the WHAT'S IN IT FOR ME ATTITUDE, BUT we must do this in a rational, responsible manner.

This morning I have shown you how PUBLIC APATHY is causing a social decline in our country; by discussing the causes, some of the effects, and some possible solutions of public apathy.

We must stop this social decline if we are to survive as a nation and to do this we must kill public apathy. In the words of Albert Nevins, "Only when individual apathy ends, will national apathy die".

INDEX